Critical Juncture:
The Future of
Peacekeeping

MICHAEL RENNER

Ann Misch, *Research Assistant*

Ed Ayres, *Editor*

WORLDWATCH PAPER 114
May 1993

THE WORLDWATCH INSTITUTE is an independent, nonprofit environmental research organization based in Washington, D.C. Its mission is to foster a sustainable society—in which human needs are met in ways that do not threaten the health of the natural environment or future generations. To this end, the Institute conducts interdisciplinary research on emerging global issues, the results of which are published and disseminated to decisionmakers and the media.

FINANCIAL SUPPORT is provided by the Geraldine R. Dodge Foundation, George Gund Foundation, W. Alton Jones Foundation, John D. and Catherine T. MacArthur Foundation, Andrew W. Mellon Foundation, Curtis and Edith Munson Foundation, Edward John Noble Foundation, Pew Charitable Trusts, Lynn R. and Karl E. Prickett Fund, Public Welfare Foundation, Rockefeller Brothers Fund, Surdna Foundation, Turner Foundation, and Frank Weeden Foundation.

PUBLICATIONS of the Institute include the annual State of the World, which is now published in 27 languages; Vital Signs, an annual compendium of the global trends—environmental, economic, and social—that are shaping our future; the Environmental Alert book series; and World Watch magazine, as well as the Worldwatch Papers. For more information on Worldwatch publications, write: Worldwatch Institute, 1776 Massachusetts Ave., N.W., Washington, DC 20036; or FAX (202) 296-7635.

THE WORLDWATCH PAPERS provide in-depth, quantitative and qualitative analysis of the major issues affecting prospects for a sustainable society. The Papers are authored by members of the Worldwatch Institute research staff and reviewed by experts in the field. Published in five languages, they have been used as a concise and authoritative reference by governments, nongovernmental organizations and educational institutions worldwide. For a partial list of available Papers, see page 75.

Table of Contents

Tables and Figures

ACKNOWLEDGEMENTS: I would like to thank Erskine Childers, William Durch, Robert Johansen, and my colleagues at Worldwatch Institute for their valuable general suggestions and for specific comments on preliminary drafts of this paper. Any remaining errors or misrepresentations are solely my responsibility. Project oversight was provided by Christopher Flavin, vice president for research at Worldwatch.

MICHAEL RENNER, a Senior Researcher at the Worldwatch Institute, studies the link between the environment and peace and security issues. He is author of a book commissioned by the United Nations Institute for Disarmament Research, *Economic Adjustments After the Cold War: Strategies for Conversion (1992),* and co-author of five of Worldwatch Institute's annual *State of the World* reports. Among the four previous Worldwatch Papers he authored are *National Security: The Economic and Environmental Dimensions* and *Swords into Plowshares: Converting to a Peace Economy.*

Prior to joining Worldwatch in 1987, he was a researcher at the World Policy Institute in New York and Corliss Lamont Fellow in Economic Conversion at Columbia University. He holds degrees in international relations and political science from the Universities of Amsterdam, the Netherlands, and Konstanz, Germany.

Introduction

In the three years since the formal end of the Cold War, the world has been rocked by a series of events as unexpectedly momentous as the East-West conflict itself: the 1991 Gulf War, the collapse of Somalia, the brutalization of Bosnia—and many others. The international community is faced with a wave of new conflicts even as it inherits from the previous era such formidable challenges as slashing the accumulated stocks of weapons and preventing the further spread of weapons of mass destruction.

Seen individually, these events pose some perplexing regional problems. Taken together, however, they amount to nothing less than an epochal watershed: a time that future historians may describe as the moment when humanity seized—or failed to seize—the opportunity to replace obsolescent mechanisms for resolving human conflict.

The traditional rule for regulating conflict and providing security was expressed by the ancient Roman maxim, *si vis pacem, para bellum*: if you want peace, prepare for war. This has been a guiding principle of nations for some 2,000 years, and it has rarely been questioned. The vast bulk of all preparation for war during these 20 centuries has been concentrated in *this* century. By the ancient logic then, the 20th century should also have produced the most stable peace. Yet, the result has been the opposite: devising ever more ingenious weapons, governments have acquired an unprecedented ability to destroy but little capacity to defend. The 20th century has produced 75 percent of all war deaths inflicted since the rise of Rome.[1]

In the ancient and medieval worlds, with relatively little commerce or communication among disparate societies and a limited reach of technology, nations were largely the masters of their own destinies. It may have made sense to seek security uni-laterally and at the expense of other nations, by building mili-tary might. But the advent of the global village has turned the ancient Romans' doctrine into an anachronistic precept: eco-nomic and environmental interdependencies among nations today are intricate, and technologies too pervasive to be confined by national boundaries.

A new principle of conflict resolution is therefore warranted: if you want peace, prepare for peace. Unless the world con-sciously replaces the ancient doctrine with a new and more effective kind of *collective* security, the post-Cold War conflicts may take on a dangerous momentum of their own.

The ending of the Cold War at first brought a wave of eupho-ria—a sense that the "major" risks of global holocaust had been averted at last, and that all that remained were various "minor" conflicts. These conflicts were treated by the one remaining superpower almost like a game, as reflected in a headline that appeared in the *Los Angeles Times* on the eve of the Gulf War: "For Troops at Border, It's Kick-off Time."[2]

But as months went by and the sharply executed, media-san-itized "Desert Storm" was replaced in the news by the grim and protracted horrors of starving children in Somalia and mutilat-ed women in Bosnia-Herzegovina, it became obvious that in some sense the world faced a very serious—and rending—new set of problems. Even the Gulf War turned out not to be a solu-tion, but a problem that largely remained once the spasm of high-tech war had subsided.

The international community has responded in different ways to each of these theaters of conflict—reflecting the lack of a consistent strategy for dealing with threats to peace in the post-Cold War world. One reason is that the post-Cold War conflicts are perplexingly different from what traditional "defense" forces are prepared for. Long-suppressed ethnic antag-onisms, suddenly unleashed, are threatening the violent disin-tegration of states. But another is that the international com-munity itself has changed, and is struggling to redefine its role in a rapidly changing world.

Far from gaining a new stability from the breaking up of the

Soviet Union, the world is being torn by contradictory trends toward globalization and fragmentation. On one hand it is being pulled together by international trade, investment, travel, and communications. On the other, it is being rocked by the reassertion of local identities and—in fearful reaction—by the rise of xenophobic and exclusivist movements. Writing in *Atlantic Monthly*, Benjamin Barber has perceptively called these opposing trends "jihad vs. McWorld." What the globalizing and the "retribalizing" dynamics have in common is that they work to erode the sovereign state—either by transcending it or by pulverizing it. Yet, formally, at least, the state remains the fundamental organizing principle of international affairs.[3]

The new instabilities are exacerbated by a range of new uncertainties—looming global issues virtually unheard of a generation or two ago. Along with accelerating population growth, nations find themselves burdened by massive degradation of human habitats and of the natural systems that underpin the livelihood of all societies. Intertwined with worsening social and economic inequities, environmental pressures could have a unifying or polarizing effect.

The international community is edging toward a greater reliance on the promise of "collective security"—in recognition of the fact that in a world of increasingly interconnected economies and communications, fortress-based forms of security are becoming more and more anachronistic. The contours of a collective security system are emerging less by design, however, than by ad hoc responses to crises around the globe. The United Nations' moves toward an alternative security system have been tentative, inconsistent, and often lacking in teeth—undermined by lack of agreement on what its powers should be, underfunded by a refusal of key members to pay all their dues, and overwhelmed by demands for services it is not fully prepared to render. As Robert Johansen of Notre Dame University's Institute for International Peace Studies has noted, the U.N. "has become essential before it has become effective."[4]

While the Persian Gulf, the Balkans, and the Horn of Africa seem to have little in common, they are now inextricably linked by history. Though separated by geography, and perhaps as disparate as imaginable in the immediate circumstances of their conflicts, they together form the crucible in which the U.N. must find a formula for making peace. How the international community handles the challenge of balancing the needs for individual human rights, tribal identity, national sovereignty, and collective security will largely determine whether the world can turn back from the dangerous path it is now following.

After the Cold War: The New Violence

The term "war" still conjures up an image of massed armies clashing on the battlefield. But this kind of war is now largely a thing of the past. The vast majority of violent disputes today (and quite likely of tomorrow) are of a different nature: civil wars in which the fighting is not limited to a delineated battlefield, and in which the distinction between combatants and non-combatants is blurred. In fact, of the more than 30 major armed conflicts active in 1992 (see Map 1), none was unambiguously of the classical country-against-country variety, and only four displayed some of its characteristics. Analysts are now more concerned with the distinctions between "state-control" conflicts (armed groups fighting to topple a government and replace it with their own) and "state-formation" conflicts (armed groups fighting to secede from a state or to gain greater autonomy within it).[5]

Still, although wars of the inter-state variety are less common, they have not become extinct; new ones could well be ignited in coming years. The fighting in the former Yugoslavia could spark a much wider Balkans conflagration; the Middle East remains a powderkeg despite intensive negotiations; and China has unresolved territorial disputes with some of its neighbors. Relations between India and Pakistan, between the two Koreas, and between Russia and some of its neighbors (Ukraine, Georgia, and the Baltic states) remain strained or uneasy.

Since 1945, some 135 wars, most of them in the developing world, have killed more than 22 million people—the equivalent of a World War III. Whether through direct casualties or war-

induced starvation or disease, civilians constitute a rapidly growing share of the victims: they accounted for half of all war-related deaths in the 1950s, three-quarters in the 1980s, and almost
90 percent in 1990.[6]

Shocking as these statistics are, they still cannot fully convey
the magnitude of the destruction inflicted on civilian life—and
on the human prospect—in the last few years. Nomads in
southern Sudan are starved to death by a combination of
drought and warfare; peasants walking in their fields in
Afghanistan have their legs blown off by land mines; and Muslim
women in Bosnia are systematically raped in front of their own
families and thus turned into victims of what *New York Times*
columnist Anna Quindlen called "psychosexual destruction."[7]

The survivors are often turned into refugees: worldwide,
there were 18 million officially recognized international refugees
in 1992 (up from 2 million in 1951), and another 20 million dis-
placed *inside* their own countries. Even if the violence that drove
them away abates, many refugees may never be able to return:
their houses are destroyed, their fields littered with explosives,
their wells poisoned, and their communities shattered.[8]

A handful of the current (or recently concluded) conflicts
stand out for their extraordinary claim on human life: the wars
in Cambodia, Afghanistan, Mozambique, and Sudan are each
estimated to have killed one million people or more. In Uganda,
Angola, and Somalia, the dead run into the hundreds of thousands. In places like Lebanon, East Timor (Indonesia), and
Guatemala, the absolute number of people killed is somewhat
lower—but relative to the small populations involved, the bloodshed is enormous.[9]

Western television audiences have become tragically famil-
iar with the "ethnic cleansing" of Bosnia and the "killing fields"
of Cambodia; Somalia and Lebanon have become synonymous
with death and destruction. But there are many more places
where no TV cameras and few outside observers are present to
provide an eyewitness report to the world. These may seem
"remote" (of no "strategic" interest), or have hard-to-pronounce
names, but the suffering is no less real, and the destruction no
less horrendous. There is fighting among Armenians and

MAP 1.
Major Armed Conflicts, 1992–93

Afghanistan
Angola
Armenia/Azerbaijan
Bangladesh
Bosnia
Burundi
Cambodia
Chad
Colombia
Croatia
Georgia
Guatemala
India
Indonesia
Iran
Iraq
Israel/Palestine
Kenya
Laos
Liberia
Myanmar (Burma)
Northern Ireland
Pakistan
Peru
Philippines
Rwanda
Somalia
South Africa
Sri Lanka
Sudan
Tajikistan
Turkey
Uganda
Western Sahara
Zaire

Equator

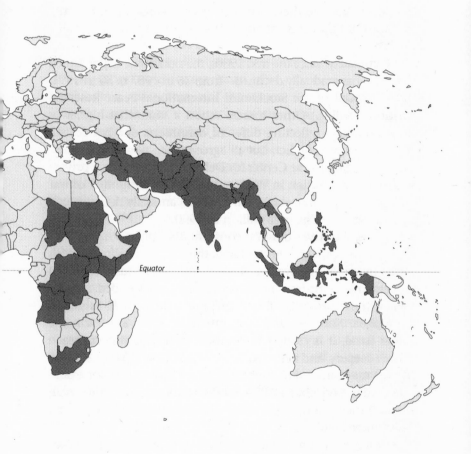

SOURCE: See note 5.

Map by Magellan Geographix^{SM}

taged; although some might be content with pressing for domestic changes in their favor, many have separatist leanings.[13]

Indeed, the post-Cold War era is coming to be haunted by the specter of violent disintegration of states. What occurred yesterday in Lebanon and is happening today in Yugoslavia, Sudan, or India may tomorrow be replicated in Russia and elsewhere. And rarely is the splitting-up of states likely to be as amicable as it was in Czechoslovakia. If the world community wishes to be more than a helpless spectator to the violent unraveling of societies, it needs to find ways either to assist multi-ethnic states to split up peacefully, or to develop a modus vivendi that allows people of different heritage to coexist peacefully.[14]

As the example of Bosnia-Herzegovina illustrates (see Map 2), ethnic groups are sometimes so interspersed that even an ingenious redrawing of borders is unlikely to produce any "pure" nation-states, but instead creates new minorities or disenfranchised populations—unless millions of people are uprooted. And partition may simply mean that an internal conflict is transformed into a war between separate states. If boundaries are to be changed at all, it is important to reinforce the principle that none be altered by violent means. Yet, the international community has not agreed on any guidelines for assuring that this principle is respected. In Africa, post-colonial governments have refrained from challenging any borders, no matter how artificial, for fear of opening a pandora's box.[15]

The alternative to creating separate states for each secessionist ethnic group is trying to make peaceful coexistence within existing boundaries work. This goal could be attained in any of three ways—each implying a different degree of interaction among ethnic groups. One is to work toward integrating ethnic groups and building a true "nation," by promoting democratic governance, fostering greater respect for human rights, and organizing the civic affairs of countries along integrative rather than divisive lines. Yet, even under the best of circumstances, such integration is a long-term endeavor.

A more immediate approach is either to grant autonomy for regions inhabited by minorities or to hammer out a power-sharing agreement among contending groups. In Lebanon, for exam-

MAP 2.

Ethnic Composition of Bosnia-Herzegovina in 1991 (before the outbreak of war)

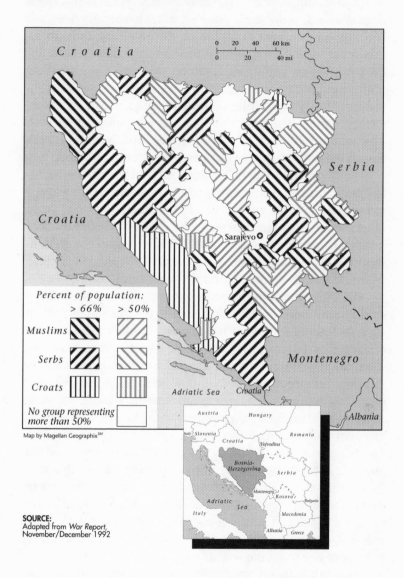

Percent of population:

	> 66%	> 50%
Muslims		
Serbs		
Croats		

No group representing
more than 50%

Map by Magellan Geographix℠

SOURCE:
Adapted from *War Report*,
November/December 1992

ple, political posts like the presidency, the premiership, and the parliamentary leadership were permanently assigned to Christians, Sunnis, and Shiites under a 1953 pact. Even once it is established, however, a power-sharing arrangement is still liable to be challenged in the future. For example, if the demographics on which the agreement was based changes substantially, the group whose population increases will expect a larger share of the pie, but the other group or groups may resist giving up some of their power. If these issues are not resolved in a satisfactory manner, the pact can unravel and disputes turn violent. This is precisely what happened in Lebanon, which in 1975 descended into nearly two decades of devastating turmoil.[16]

The alternative to diversity, pluralism, and tolerance is relentless bloodshed. If resentments across cultural divides are allowed to fester, even trivial grievances and imagined injustices can be magnified to the point where, in the eye of the beholder, they justify the resort to violence. As the former Yugoslavia demonstrates, it is all too easy for political leaders to play on people's fears and fuel the flames of exclusivist passions.

The U.N. cannot be expected to make diversity work in the world's many sovereign states; the primary responsibility falls on each individual society within its own borders. But without outside prodding or assistance, some societies may fail. The international community has a stake in exploring ways that it can help to foster greater harmony within societies, establish adequate protections for minorities, and promote more equitable patterns of economic development to make relations among different nationalities less of a zero-sum game. Writing about Bosnia's prewar "extraordinary amalgam of ethnicities, religions [and] cultures," Zoran Pajic argues in *War Report,* "this cosmopolitanism stands as a threatening obstacle to the idea of intolerant Balkan nation-states.... If the international community cannot salvage this Bosnian identity it will show itself incapable of confronting the process of violent disintegration in the rest of the changing world."[17]

Thus, while the overall number of major wars has declined in recent years, it is not at all clear that this downturn will continue. In fact, a compilation by the Carter Center in Atlanta,

Georgia, shows an upturn in the number from 1991 to 1992. The future may well bring a new surge of warfare. An analysis including "lesser" conflicts actually shows a steady increase in the number of violent conflicts throughout the post-World War II period. The occurrence of violent conflict will not diminish unless the world community confronts the root causes, directing adequate attention and resources to conflict prevention at the earliest stages possible. The current international system encourages, even compels, each state and each contender to arm itself against perceived or real opponents. The widespread availability of arms and the lack of an alternative, non-violent system for the settlement of conflicts virtually invite recourse to coercive means.[18]

If war is to lose its legitimacy as an acceptable instrument in the conduct of human affairs, the still feeble norms against the use of force need to be reinforced, and global institutions that can promote peaceful conflict resolution need to be bolstered. Among the key components of an alternative system are a shift from offensive weapons and strategies to ones that can defend but not attack, and a strengthening of international peacekeeping and peacemaking capacities. But if peacekeeping and peacemaking are to succeed, they need to be accompanied by meaningful barriers against the production, possession, trade, and use of armaments. There is, in short, a symbiotic relationship between international peacekeeping and disarmament.

Reducing the Availability of Arms

Unrestrained production and trading of arms has resulted in enough accumulation of weapons around the world to ensure that fighting, once it breaks out, can continue for a long time. Spending an estimated $30 trillion (in 1990 dollars) for military purposes since World War II, the world's nations have acquired a collective arsenal of unprecedented lethality. In 1992, they had either deployed or stockpiled some 45,000 combat aircraft, 172,000 main battle tanks, 155,000 artillery pieces, more than 1,000 major surface warships, and about 700 military submarines. Added to these are tens of thousands of light tanks, armored vehicles, helicopters, mortars, missiles, and smaller naval vessels. Assault rifles, machine guns, and other small arms, meanwhile, are far too abundant to keep track of. Although the bulk of these armaments (and especially the most sophisticated pieces of weaponry) are found in the Northern industrialized countries, many developing countries, particularly those in Asia and the Middle East, have built substantial military machines of their own. Few of them produce weapons domestically, but a huge arms trade keeps them well-supplied. Since 1960, at least $1 trillion dollars worth of arms crossed international borders, much of it going to the Third World.[19]

Although armaments are often just a symptom of unresolved deeper conflicts, there are three reasons why curbing their availability is nevertheless crucial. First, the proliferation of arms frequently does gain a momentum of its own. Governments argue that they simply want to maintain a balance of power with their adversaries, but they are unlikely to be satisfied with an equilibrium. In a heavily-armed world, each adversary is likely to see its opponent's capabilities and intentions through the lens of a worst-case scenario, and therefore be more inclined to build up its own military muscle. There is usually no agreement on what constitutes true parity, and the result is an imbalance that drives an escalating arms race—such as that being waged between India and Pakistan, for example.[20]

Second, the ready availability of arms often means that governments rely on them to settle disputes with other governments or domestic opponents—if not by their actual use, by threatened use—rather than on the admittedly difficult compromises without which lasting political solutions and a stable peace are impossible. In both the Israeli-Arab struggle and the recently terminated civil war in El Salvador, for example, the steady infusion of arms from politically interested suppliers kept conflicts fueled for years.[21]

Third, limiting arms is essential because where they are ubiquitous—as they are in many countries—the outbreak of hostilities tends to have much more devastating consequences than if they were less widely available. Somalia is a case in point.

Large amounts of arms were supplied during the Cold War, first by the Soviet Union and then by the United States, each in its efforts to draw the country into its sphere of influence. In the civil war that broke out in 1991, Somalia's infrastructure has been destroyed, its economy collapsed, and government authority disintegrated. Status and power now are obtained at gunpoint, with armed factions ruthlessly competing for spoils. Keeping or imposing peace in such a situation is fraught with difficulty.[22]

Preparing for peace rather than for war requires a sharp break with past practice. Many "peacetime" military activities are not subject to any international rules. And where they exist, treaties have often been guided by the philosophy of arms *control*, which is aimed at managing arms races and allows arsenals to expand as long as "stability" is maintained. By contrast, a disarmament approach seeks deep reductions or even elimination of weapons.

> **The few controls that have been put in place have typically limited the deployment— but not the production—of weapons systems.**

Until recently, arms control agreements—particularly those concerning nuclear weapons—have been carefully tailored to establish weak limits only for aging or redundant weapons systems, thus allowing an unabated buildup. And since many treaties have failed to limit the size of existing arsenals, few contain any provision to destroy even part of the accumulated stockpiles. Even more ominously, these treaties have been concerned only with the *quantities* of weapons, with no constraints on the development of ever more sophisticated technologies of destruction. And the few controls that have been put in place have typically limited the *deployment*—but not the *production*—of weapons systems. (See Table 1.) With the exception of the 1993 Chemical Weapons Convention (CWC), which stipulates that production facilities be demolished, none of the existing treaties includes a mandate to dismantle or convert arms factories to civilian use.[23]

A corollary to the focus on arms control as opposed to disarmament is the Western emphasis on *nonproliferation* of nuclear,

TABLE 1.

Constraints Imposed on Armaments by International Treaties[1]

Treaty Name (Year Signed)	Constraints					Requirement
	Production	Possession/ Deployment	Exports/ Transfers	Use	Testing	Destruction of Stocks
NUCLEAR WEAPONS						
Test treaties[2]					O	
Tlatelolco (1967)	●	●	●	●	●	
Non-Proliferation (1968)[3]	O	O	●			
SALT I/II (1972/79)	O	O			O	O[4]
Rarotonga (1985)	●	●	●	●	●	
INF (1988)	●	●			●	●
START I/II (1991/1993)	O	O	●		O	O[4]
WEAPONS OF MASS DESTRUCTION[5]						
Outer Space Treaty (1967)		●			●	
Seabed Treaty (1971)		●		●	●	
Moon Treaty (1979)		●		●	●	
CHEMICAL/BIOLOGICAL WEAPONS						
Geneva Protocol (1925)				●		
Biological Weapons Convention (1972)	●	●	●	●	●	●
U.S.-Soviet Chemical Weapons (1990)	●	O				O
Chemical Weapons Convention (1993)	●	●		●		●
CONVENTIONAL WEAPONS						
Conventional Forces in Europe (1990)		O				O
Inhumane Weapons Convention (1981)				O/●[6]		
BALLISTIC MISSILES						
Anti-Ballistic Missile Treaty (1972)	O	O	●		O	O
Missile Technology Control Regime (1987)[7]			O			

[1]"●" means a total ban, "O" a partial ban or limitation. The table presents constraints imposed by the treaties, but not the effectiveness with which they are enforced. [2]Partial Test Ban Treaty (1963), Threshold Test Ban Treaty (1974), Peaceful Nuclear Explosions Treaty (1976). [3]The prohibitions against production and possession are partial in the sense that they apply to non- nuclear states, but not to nuclear-weapon states. [4]Launch vehicles or silos only, not warheads. [5]Includes nuclear and non-nuclear types. [6]Use of certain types of weapons banned altogether, that of others restricted. [7]The MTCR is an export control cartel of Western suppliers.

SOURCE: Worldwatch Institute, based on sources cited in note 23.

chemical, and biological weapons and modern military technologies. Nonproliferation would seem like a commendable
goal; the spreading of lethal technology cannot be desirable.
Yet unless coupled with unambiguous moves toward *disarmament* among the world's strongest military powers, the approach
suggests that the "haves" are more interested in maintaining a
system of global military apartheid—preventing the "have-nots"
from acquiring military capabilities others already possess—
than in finding a way to make the planet less heavily armed and
more secure. If that is the case, nonproliferation efforts may
well thwart the chances for a more cooperative approach to
international security. They feed into Third World resentment,
not least because the technologies in question often can be used
not just for military but also for civilian purposes. In the long
run, attempts to prevent the spread of advanced military technologies will work only if restrictions against their development
and application are accepted equally by North and South.[24]

Only with the thawing of the Cold War were greater
restraints put in place. Whereas the Strategic Arms Limitation
Talks (SALT) treaties of the 1970s let the superpowers pile up huge
quantities of nuclear warheads, the 1988 Intermediate-Range
Nuclear Forces (INF) accord and the 1991 and 1993 Strategic
Arms Reductions Talks agreements (START I and II) begin to
cut them. The Conventional Forces in Europe (CFE) treaty is leading to sizable reductions of tanks and artillery on that continent.
And the CWC will outlaw the production and possession of
toxic agents, and require the destruction of existing stockpiles.[25]

After growing seemingly inexorably for more than four
decades, nuclear arsenals now are set for a substantial shrinkage,
and the production of weapons-grade fissile materials and the
testing of new warheads has declined substantially. Still, the
agreed cuts would only return the warhead numbers to the level
they were at in 1968—the year when the Nuclear Non-
Proliferation Treaty was signed and the atomic powers pledged
to seriously move toward nuclear disarmament. The remaining
stockpile will still contain sufficient firepower to annihilate all
life on earth. Although none of the nuclear powers is contem-
plating the eventual abolition of nuclear weapons, going to

zero may be the only way to prevent their growing spread. Continued possession of nuclear weapons by a few "haves" lends legitimacy to other countries' efforts to acquire them. As long as possession of a nuclear arsenal is perceived to have political or military value, and to confer special status and diplomatic leverage, it is almost certain that more governments will attempt to join the club—and may well succeed.[26]

What the world community has still failed to achieve in the nuclear realm, it appears to have accomplished in the sphere of chemical arms. After years of arduous negotiations, a multilateral Chemical Weapons Convention was opened for signature in January 1993. It will come into force 180 days after it has been ratified by 65 countries, but no sooner than January 1995. The 1925 Geneva Protocol had prohibited the use of chemical and biological means of warfare, but not their production and possession. The CWC closes this crucial gap and mandates the destruction of all existing stocks as well as the dismantling of all production facilities within 10 years. Meanwhile, the 1972 Biological Weapons Convention contains the same prohibitions as the chemical treaty, but in marked contrast lacks a precise definition of the prohibited items and has no effective verification or enforcement measures. Efforts to strengthen it are continuing.[27]

Proliferation concerns notwithstanding, the number of countries that possess nuclear, chemical, or biological arsenals, or are thought to be both interested in and capable of acquiring them, is quite small—perhaps no more than two dozen. By contrast, the spread of conventional weapons is, as their name suggests, nearly universal. And while nuclear arms have the potential to wipe out all of humanity, it is of course conventional arms that are the stock of conflicts. Yet, little progress is in sight with regard to constraints against their manufacture, trade, and use.

Some headway has been made with the 1990 CFE Treaty. Signed by the members of the North Atlantic Treaty Organization (NATO) and the now-dissolved Warsaw Pact, it established equal limits on the numbers of battle tanks, armored vehicles, artillery pieces, combat aircraft, and helicopters that the states in the area—reaching from the Atlantic to the Ural Mountains—may deploy. Implementing the Treaty means that one of the most militarized regions of the world will need to weed out its immense arsenals. Even so, large numbers of arms, particularly the most sophisticated kinds, will remain on the continent. The treaty, in any event, does not erect any hurdles to continued weapons modernization.[28]

The limitations of the CFE Treaty notwithstanding, the European experience stands in striking contrast with the situation in many other regions, particularly the Third World, where numerous unresolved conflicts continue to fuel arms races. An important step toward defusing these would be to curb the flow of arms across borders. The Third World currently accounts for about 60 percent of world arms imports, and most of these countries depend almost entirely on imports for equipping their armed forces. Fewer weapons imports would likely improve the level of trust among opponents and provide an opening for peaceful settlement. In the few instances where developing countries possess a significant domestic arms manufacturing capacity, import restraints would need to be matched with production restraints.[29]

The Third World now accounts for about 60 percent of world arms imports.

Throughout the past half-century, attempts to curb the international arms trade have been unsuccessful. In keeping with the traditional balance-of-power approach, virtually all governments assert that arms transfers—especially their own—can help create stability in relations among countries. The decline in arms exports that has occurred since the mid-1980s is a result not of political restraint but of dire economic conditions: many developing countries cannot afford to continue their buying binge. This means a reversal of economic fortunes could revive the flow of weaponry. Thus, while the end of the Cold War creates an opportunity to remove the link between arms exports and big-power influence peddling, ideological factors are now often replaced by economic considerations. As domestic military procurement budgets shrink in East and West, many arms producers see their best hope in aggressively pursuing export markets. In the absence of adequate programs to convert weapons production facilities to civilian use, this pressure will continue.[30]

A number of countries have adopted national arms export regulations, with relatively little constraining effect. The few international attempts to curb arms exports remain halfhearted. For instance, the largest arms exporters—the United States, Russia, China, the United Kingdom, and France—have been talking about restraining arms sales for two years. But to date they have only produced vaguely worded statements, the interpretation of which has been left to each government. For example, they endorsed transfers "conducted in a responsible manner."[31]

Although supplier restraint is crucial, controls are unlikely to work in today's buyer's market without comparable commitments by recipient nations. Whether on a bilateral or regional basis, self-imposed quantitative ceilings on weapons imports would yield a mutual reduction of tensions—and economic burdens. An even better approach, however—since some countries have the capability to produce arms domestically and hence rely less on imports—would be to prohibit the deployment of specific weapon systems, or to establish weapons-free zones. To date, however, there has been a conspicuous lack of recipient initiatives.[32]

Greater transparency about arms transfers and other military matters can help build the confidence among governments needed to reduce arms. An encouraging initiative in this regard is the effort to establish an international arms trade register. A December 1991 U.N. General Assembly resolution asked all governments to voluntarily submit, on an annual basis, information concerning transfers of major weapons systems. Data for the calendar year 1992 were to be made available by April 1993. Initially, at least, the register includes only a small number of items and the reporting requirements are not highly detailed. No distinctions are made, for example, about the technical sophistication of weapons. And the 1992 *SIPRI Yearbook* comments that the register "will not report on those areas of the arms trade about which least is known—deliveries of small arms, components, sub-systems and arms production technologies and dual-use items."[33]

Over time, these shortcomings may be corrected; the register's scope could be expanded when it comes up for review in 1994. One possibility is to include arms production—an idea favored by many developing countries. To make the system effective, national reporting will need to be made mandatory, with international inspectors verifying data submitted. The register could then become, in time, a tool not just to monitor arms flows but to curb them. However, governments will need to grow comfortable with a voluntary approach first—and to be persuaded that the reporting does indeed serve a useful purpose. As such confidence takes hold, the scope and authority of the register can be gradually broadened.[34]

As domestic military procurement budgets shrink in East and West, many arms producers see their best hope in aggressively pursuing export markets.

True demilitarization can only occur with international agreements that impose strict limits on military arsenals. Such agreements, in turn, can only be concluded and implemented if there is confidence that all nations will adhere to the terms. And the necessary trust requires the existence of a comprehensive verification and inspection system. Verification begins with data exchanges and "baseline" inspections to establish a reliable inventory of existing arsenals. The destruction of weapons is then monitored. At the same time, continuous on-site and remote monitoring of declared weapons development and production facilities, and challenge inspections at any suspect sites, help ensure that the manufacturing of arms is not resumed. It is equally important that enforcement provisions, such as sanctions, are established.[35]

During the Cold War years, on-site inspections of military facilities were generally unacceptable to governments intent on maintaining military secrets. During the Gorbachev years, the

Soviet Union, wanting to end the confrontation with the West, became much more accommodating to such inspections. In the meantime, technological advances and greater political acceptance of intrusive measures have combined to boost the role of verification. The INF, START, CFE, and CWC accords all incorporate extensive and detailed arrangements for such monitoring and verification activities.[36]

As a result of these treaties, the NATO states and the former members of the Warsaw Pact all have national pools of qualified inspection personnel. Yet, for future accords, it would be useful to establish a well-endowed and competently staffed international disarmament verification agency. Inspectors accountable to an international organization tend to be more acceptable than those employed by a national government because they are viewed as less likely to engage in espionage. In any case, many developing countries would be hard-pressed to marshal the trained personnel and sophisticated technologies—and the financial resources—needed for this purpose.[37]

It is crucial that the world's nations gain more experience with far-reaching verification measures. For arsenals to be slashed more deeply or eliminated altogether, governments need to develop confidence that such measures will enhance, not undermine, security. They need to be certain that there is a dependable alternative to the competitive buildup of national military prowess, and that nonviolent means to resolve conflicts can be effective. That alternative can be found in the still embryonic but rapidly evolving international peacekeeping and peacemaking services of the United Nations.

U.N. Peacekeeping: Promise and Peril

With the ending of the East-West confrontation, the United Nations may finally become what its founders envisioned: an organization at the center of a collective security system. When U.N. peacekeepers were awarded the Nobel Peace Prize in 1988, Secretary-General Javier Pérez de Cuéllar noted that it marked the first time in history that "military forces have been

employed internationally not to wage war, not to establish dom-
ination and not to serve the interests of any power or group of
powers."[38]

Curiously enough, peacekeeping—as presently practiced by
the U.N. "Blue Helmets"—is an accident of history. Originally,
the Security Council was to have had, on call, a full-strength
armed force assembled from national armies of member states,
for the purpose of "maintaining international peace and security." But the Cold War rivalry between the United States and
the Soviet Union deadlocked the Security Council (neither side
was willing to have the U.N. intervene against its own allies or
in its sphere of influence), and the provisions of Article 43 of the
U.N. Charter were never implemented. An improvised alternative—peacekeeping with no combat capability—arose in its
place. "The vision of the United Nations was downsized from
world policeman to world volunteer fire brigade," says Jeff
Laurenti of the private United Nations Association of the United
States (UNA-USA). "To a very considerable degree, the founders'
expectation of a muscular U.N. that would provide for the common defense was strangled in the cradle."[39]

Improvisation turned this weakness into a virtue, however.
Instead of enforcing the will of the Security Council by simply
becoming another combatant trying to outgun any opponent,
the U.N. found that it could succeed by adhering to nonviolent
principles. This non-aggressive approach was adopted as a general policy, with peacekeeping troops using their light weapons
only in self-defense. Now, before any peacekeeping forces are dispatched, the combatants must first agree to cease hostilities and
consent to any U.N. deployment. A crucial element in mar-
shaling the support of both the major powers and the local
antagonists has been the U.N.'s reputation for impartiality, its
being an "honest broker."

In the first four decades of U.N. peacekeeping, only 14 operations were undertaken. In recent years, however, the Blue
Helmets have been inundated with requests for their services.
The past five years have witnessed as many new operations as the
previous four decades—including the three largest ever undertaken, in Cambodia, Yugoslavia, and Somalia. (See Table 2.) In

TABLE 2.
Budgets and Personnel of Recent and Ongoing U.N. Peacekeeping Operations and Observer Missions

UN Operation Place	Duration	Budget[1] ($ million)	Personnel[2]
Israel/Egypt/Lebanon/Syria	since 1948	31	259
India/Pakistan	since 1949	5	39
Cyprus	since 1964	31	2,197
Golan Heights	since 1974	43	1,120
Lebanon	since 1978	157	5,643
Afghanistan/Pakistan	1988-90	7	50
Iran/Iraq	1988-91	9	750
Namibia	1989-90	410	6,150
Nicaragua	1989-90	2	494
Central America	1989-92	26	625
Angola	since 1989[3]	52	298[4]
Haiti	1990	5	312
El Salvador	since 1991	70	530[5]
Iraq/Kuwait	since 1991	67	353[6]
Western Sahara	since 1991	59	332[7]
Cambodia	since 1991	1,700	18,901[8]
Croatia/Bosnia/Macedonia	since 1992	607	22,063[9]
Somalia	since 1992[10]	1,550	30,800
Mozambique	since 1992	332	7,500[11]

[1]UN peacekeeping operations are not budgeted on a fiscal or calendar year basis but for a period of time that can be shorter than a full year or stretch from one year into the next. The figures reported here represent the most recent period of time applicable. [2]At year-end 1992. Including soldiers, military observers, police, election monitors, civilian experts (composition differs from operation to operation). [3]Authorized until May 31, 1993; may be extended. [4]Authorized strength: 350 military observers and 126 police monitors. [5]Authorized strength: 1,000 military and police personnel and 146 civilian staff. [6]Authorized strength: 3,645. [7]Authorized strength: 1,603 military observers and troops, 300 police officers, and 800-1,000 civilian personnel. [8]Planned full strength: 22,000. [9]Of which about 7,500 in Bosnia, and 750 (observers only) in Macedonia. [10]Before May 1993, the U.N. presence was limited to a 550-strong force. [11]Authorized strength; not reached yet.

SOURCE: Worldwatch Institute, based on sources cited in note 40.

some cases, such as Namibia or the Western Sahara, stalemate and war weariness have driven the combatants to embrace the U.N. as a peacemaker. In others, the former Cold War adversaries approached governments they had been supporting, and pressured them to make concessions in order to settle long-standing disputes.[40]

For many years, peacekeeping operations focused narrowly on conflict containment—monitoring borders and buffer zones after cease-fires were signed, as happened on the Golan Heights between Israel and Syria. But since the late 1980s, they have begun to move beyond these confines. Missions have become far more complex and ambitious—supervising the disarming or disbanding of armed factions, establishing protected areas, monitoring elections and human rights records, and repatriating refugees. They have even included—in Cambodia and now Somalia—temporarily taking over the administration of an entire nation torn by war. In such cases the U.N. has been asked to reach far beyond its original mission, by facilitating the rebuilding of institutions and infrastructures, and thus the rebirth of civilian society. And now, with the new mission in Somalia (perhaps soon to be repeated in Bosnia), U.N. forces have for the first time been authorized to impose peace and, if necessary, to forcibly disarm warring factions. In effect, peace *keeping* is gradually being transformed into peace *making* and peace *enforcement*.

Since 1948, more than 650,000 people—military, police, and civilian personnel—have served in peacekeeping missions at one time or another. The $8.3 billion that the United Nations spent on peacekeeping from 1948 to 1992 is a trifling fraction—less than three one-hundredths of one percent—of the roughly $30 trillion devoted to traditional military purposes over the same period. With operations growing in both number and size, annual U.N. peacekeeping outlays have risen from $233 million in 1987 to some $1.4 billion in 1992—still only about as much as the U.S. Air Force spent that year to purchase 48 F-16 jet fighters. But this tiny commitment appears to be due for explosive expansion. It will continue to rise in 1993, with a much enlarged operation in Somalia likely to cost $1.5 billion. If an enforcement effort is undertaken in Bosnia, it may cost another $3 billion. In the past three years alone, the number of people participating in U.N. operations has surged from 10,500 to about 60,000, and it will likely rise toward 100,000 during 1993. An enlarged Bosnia operation would require at least 50,000 troops.[41]

This explosion of responsibilities threatens to overwhelm the small peacekeeping staff. Describing the worsening communications bottlenecks that compel "force commanders [to] ring me up at home during the weekend for instructions and find the phone is busy," Kofi Annan, the U.N.'s top peacekeeping official, says "the days of gifted amateurism are over." The U.N. is now preparing to set up a permanent planning office and an operations center that allows headquarters to be in contact with all field operations 24 hours a day—a rather belated improvement for a force that has been serving off-and-on for nearly half a century! In 1992, a staff of 15 people at U.N. headquarters in New York was responsible for overseeing tens of thousands of peacekeepers in more than a dozen locations. That staff is being expanded to 50—but still hardly adequate.[42]

The rapidly rising demand for the U.N.'s services suggests that on the whole, U.N. peacekeeping has been fairly successful. It was the peacekeepers, for example, whose patrols in the demilitarized zone between Greek and Turkish Cypriots helped prevent the outbreak of renewed fighting; who verified the withdrawal of foreign troops from Angola and Namibia; and who facilitated the peaceful political transition in Nicaragua. Among the current operations, however, at least a few—in Angola, Cambodia, and the former Yugoslavia—have encountered protracted difficulties—reflecting fundamental weaknesses in the peacekeeping forces as now constituted. (See Table 3.) In some of these theaters of conflict, it is not just a lack of management support back in New York, but an overall lack of equipment and personnel in the field that has gutted the peacekeeping effort. In other cases, diplomats have been woefully unrealistic in their estimates of how long the job would take.[43]

What it takes to defuse a conflict is, in most cases, a larger and more extended U.N. presence than Security Council members have been willing to authorize. Experience in Angola and

Cambodia, in particular, has made it clear that for peacekeepers to ensure that the terms of peace pacts are implemented, they have to have enough muscle and time to substantially disarm and demobilize warring factions. Where the combatants renege on their own commitments to observe a cease-fire or disarm, the U.N. is left with the alternatives of cajoling them to honor their pledges, withdrawing, or attempting to enforce the terms agreed to—a capacity the organization does not now have, but seems to be edging toward.

But beyond the problem of its relative unpreparedness for the particular challenges of Bosnia and Cambodia, there is a more endemic set of problems that not only undermines the U.N.'s effectiveness today but could condemn it to failure in the long run. These begin with the *ad hoc* quality of the peacekeeping system itself—and are then greatly exacerbated by the changing nature of conflicts in the post-Cold War world.

Having evolved through improvisation, the current system is handicapped in a number of ways. Peacekeeping units are assembled for specific missions only, from contingents of national armed forces made available by member governments. If governments are unwilling or slow to provide contingents, the U.N.'s ability to dispatch a force speedily is severely compromised. Yet, speed can be essential to the success of a mission; cease-fires are often fragile, and the willingness of all parties to accept outsiders may evaporate quickly. Once a mission is established, the governments providing the troops may exercise an unwarranted influence over operations, or withdraw their troops on short notice. Training peacekeepers is also left to the contributing governments, resulting in uneven levels of preparation, experience and competence. Perhaps the most serious impediment is that even the financing is ad hoc; there is no regular, permanent budget for peacekeeping, and most member states either fail to pay their assessed share of costs or pay late. During

> **Even the financing is ad hoc; there is no regular, permanent budget for peacekeeping.**

TABLE 3.

Difficulties and Shortcomings of U.N. Peacekeeping: Selected Cases

Location	Observation
Cyprus	U.N. patrols demarcation zone between Greek and Turkish Cypriots. Prevented outbreak of any new fighting since 1974, but division of the island has not come any closer to being reversed. Territorial and refugee issues remain unresolved. Greek Cypriots want continued U.N. presence as a shield against the militarily stronger Turkish Cypriots, but are losing interest in reunification with economically weaker Turkish areas. Countries contributing troops to U.N. force have absorbed huge costs and are threatening to withdraw their soldiers.
Angola	U.N. supervised 1991 cease-fire and monitored 1992 elections. UNITA rebels lost elections (described by observers as fair) and resumed civil war in late 1992. In retrospect, the timetable established by the peace accord (brokered by Portugal, not the U.N.) turned out to be too constrained: elections were held before the disarmament and demobilization process was fully implemented—a mistake the U.N. is now trying to avoid repeating in Mozambique. The U.N. presence is far too small to influence the turn of events.
Western Sahara	Morocco's claim to Western Sahara contested by Polisario Front. U.N. was to prepare for referendum on independence planned for January 1992. Morocco moved settlers into the area, repeatedly violated cease-fire, and blocked U.N. voter registration efforts. U.N. has no mandate to force Moroccan compliance, and the mission's financing and personnel levels are inadequate.
Cambodia	Under the terms of an October 1991 peace treaty, U.N. is to supervise cease-fire between government and rebel groups, disarm factions, monitor human rights record, repatriate refugees (mostly accomplished), and organize and conduct elections. But cease-fire is frequently being violated. Khmer Rouge guerrillas refuse to grant U.N. access to areas under their control, have failed to disarm, and threaten to boycott elections. Government intimidating opposition groups. U.N. has neither the means nor the mandate to force compliance; its reputation is rapidly getting tarnished. Despite growing doubts whether elections can be held as early as planned (May 1993), U.N. appears determined to push them through. Most peacekeepers are expected to leave within weeks of the elections, even though civil war may resume. Reconstruction, crucial to peace, has barely begun.

TABLE 3. continued

Location	Observation
Croatia	January 1992 cease-fire between Croats and Serbs brought deployment of U.N. peacekeepers. U.N. was to facilitate return of some Serb-occupied areas to Croatian control, repatriate Croatian refugees, and oversee withdrawal of all armed forces from Serbian areas. Serbs refused to implement the peace plan; frustration over the lack of progress led Croatia to break the cease-fire in January 1993 in local fighting. Neither side is satisfied with the U.N. presence, but neither can do without it. A U.N. withdrawal would open the door to renewed full-scale war.
Bosnia	Before the Bosnian conflict erupted, the government called unsuccessfully for international monitors. When Bosnia was recognized as an independent state in April 1992 (and Bosnian Serbs started their attacks), the U.N. Security Council discussed sending 10,000 peacekeeping troops. But none were sent. A Council resolution imposing a no-fly zone over Bosnia remains unenforced. U.N. forces have no peace to keep (and neither the mandate nor the capacity to impose a peace); delivery of humanitarian aid is being thwarted by Serbs. The U.N. is faced with unpalatable alternatives of evacuating Muslim civilians besieged by Serb forces—in effect facilitating the Serb campaign of "ethnic cleansing"—or of abandoning them. A plan to divide Bosnia among the contending ethnic groups has been accepted by Croats and Muslims but rejected by the Serbs; if accepted, it would require 50,000 or more U.N. peacekeepers to guarantee compliance.
Somalia	International neglect continued even as civil war tore the country apart and triggered mass starvation. Inertia among U.N. specialized agencies led to failure to prepare emergency aid plans. U.N.'s diplomatic initiatives to end the fighting in early 1992 were bungled. Later, the dispatch of a 500-strong peacekeeping force to facilitate delivery of relief aid was delayed for months by objections of a Somali warlord and the U.S. government. An additional 3,500 peacekeepers were approved by the Security Council but not deployed for lack of resources. In May 1993, a 30,800-person U.N. peacekeeping force replaced a U.S.-led military force that had intervened in December 1992 to create conditions more favorable to the unimpeded delivery of food supplies. Somalia's warring factions agreed in late March 1993 on a plan for disarming and forming a transitional government. The U.N. now has the daunting task of disarming warlords, resettling 2.5 million refugees, and helping to rebuild the country's economic and political foundation.

SOURCE: Worldwatch Institute, based on sources cited in note 43.

the Cold War, the Soviet Union refused to pay for peacekeeping missions it did not strongly support. During the 1980s, the United States piled up hundreds of millions of dollars in arrears as the Reagan Administration and Congress deliberately reduced their payments to force changes in how the world organization operates.[44]

The case-by-case nature of this half-century-old practice persists because even though the world is asking more of its peacekeepers now, by and large it is still *reacting* to crises rather than trying to *prevent* them. This was the only approach feasible during the Cold War years. Now that the Security Council is no longer permanently deadlocked, however, preventive diplomacy is not only possible but necessary.

Preventing the eruption of disputes into full-scale hostilities is by no means an easy task, but its difficulties pale beside those of ending them once large-scale bloodshed has occurred and antipathies have been aroused and unleashed. Early recognition and defusion of emerging crises is crucial to resolving conflicts peacefully, but the U.N. still lacks appropriate tools and mechanisms.

While the peacekeeping role evolved mainly in response to conflicts between nations, the U.N. now finds itself increasingly drawn into mediating internal conflicts as well. Ten of the 15 missions begun since 1988, including those in El Salvador, Namibia, Somalia, and Cambodia, were charged with helping to resolve conflicts within rather than among countries. This raises a hornet's nest of legal and operational complications, because while the U.N.'s involvement in these cases was sought and agreed to by all parties, such consent may not always be given in the future. Article 2 of the U.N. Charter specifies that the United Nations is not authorized "to intervene in matters which are essentially within the domestic jurisdiction of any state." But the traditional distinction between internal and international affairs is becoming increasingly blurred. Civil strife within a country may have greater repercussions beyond its borders than in the past. Not only are outside powers often drawn into the conflict because they want to affect the political outcome, but ever larger streams of refugees threaten to destabilize neighboring countries, and today's far greater economic interdependence means that the fighting may have more pronounced effects in other nations.

The internal-versus-international distinction has also been eroded by the "CNN effect." Television images of massive human suffering in places like Iraq, Somalia, and Bosnia, caused either by government repression or by the collapse of civilian authority, have fueled the demand for intervention to protect human rights or to permit the provision of humanitarian aid. In effect, the growing *familiarity* of those who keep turning up in the news—whether they be emaciated children in Somalia or prisoners of war in Bosnia—transforms them from subjects of a remote and "foreign" land to fellow members of a common human society. One result of these trends is that the idea of national sovereignty must increasingly compete with that of simple human community. Intervention is perceived by the world as less like invasion, and more like rescue.[45]

In the traditional interpretation of international law, states were accorded virtually absolute primacy—which meant that even severe violations of human rights did not justify outside intervention. This rule, of course, was intended to guard against acts of aggression under the pretext of humanitarian intentions.[46]

Abdullahi Ahmed An-Na'im, a scholar at Uppsala University in Sweden, argues that national sovereignty is the manifestation of the right to self-determination in the sense that it provides an umbrella under whose protection human dignity and material well-being can be pursued. But, he says, "sovereignty loses its meaning and justification if it is used to defeat its own legitimate ends, or to protect the perpetrator of human rights violations." In other words, while sovereignty provides the legal foundation to protect weaker states against intervention by stronger ones in the international system, similar protections are needed within societies.[47]

There is growing support for the argument that the principle of national sovereignty should be superseded in cases of extreme violations of human rights or democratic principles—such as in Haiti or Myanmar. For example, in its Santiago

Declaration of 1991, the Organization of American States expressed the view that the elimination of democracy in a member country is not just an internal matter but threatens collective security. U.N. Secretary-General Boutros Boutros-Ghali recently spoke of a "dimension of universal sovereignty that resides in all humanity and provides all peoples with legitimate involvement in issues affecting the world as a whole." Sovereignty, while never absolute in reality, is coming to be seen in more relative terms, and in terms of balancing states' rights and responsibilities.[48]

Not surprisingly, humanitarian intervention is far from universally accepted. Third World governments are eager to guard their hard-won sovereignty, often suspecting that ostensibly humanitarian motives may turn out to be a convenient pretext for old-style intervention. Such suspicion is well-founded: the Western powers now dominating the U.N. Security Council have long condoned or ignored human rights violations when it was convenient to do so, as it was in El Salvador, Haiti, or South Africa. Human rights concerns are still applied selectively. For instance, the severe repression of Iraqi Kurds (belatedly) led the United States and its allies to create a safe haven in northern Iraq, while the mistreatment of Kurds in Turkey (a key Western ally in the Middle East), though less severe, has received little attention. A similar selectivity can be found in the international community's response to human suffering triggered by the violent disintegration of societies. While Somalia's plight has (belatedly) attracted world attention, comparable conditions in nearby Sudan have gone virtually unnoticed.[49]

To avoid abuse and double standards, Edward Luck and Tobi Trister Gati of the UNA-USA suggest that "over time, it may be useful to try to develop generally applicable rules of intervention... For example, specific kinds of events, threats, or situations might automatically trigger Security Council action." Such rules would legitimize no unilateral action—only action by the U.N. This would offer some assurance that humanitarian intervention is dictated not by the narrow political or economic interests of a powerful government or corporation but by a universal concern for human dignity.[50]

Restoring the peace inside a country wracked by conflict is a more treacherous undertaking than monitoring international borders. Government troops, insurgents, and factions competing for power confront peacekeepers with a tangle of self-proclaimed authorities. As the situation in Bosnia illustrates, protagonists may deliberately leave the outside world confused about who controls the acts of militias and other irregular armed groups. To try to compel some of these groups to adhere to cease-fires, unmolested passage of humanitarian aid convoys, or inspections of prisoners-of-war camps can easily pull peacekeepers into a quagmire.

The traditional peacekeeping model is based on the principles of impartiality, nonviolence, consent of all parties, and no deployment without an established cease-fire. It is workable in cases where the U.N. is called upon by the warring parties themselves to police a cease-fire. But it appears unworkable in the two types of situations that the U.N. is increasingly getting involved in: those in which it is invited to facilitate a demilitarization but the combatants fail to comply with the terms they earlier agreed to; and those in which it intervenes against the express wishes of one or more of the contenders, for humanitarian purposes.

The peacekeeping model was never really meant to apply to situations like those in which Bosnian women are systematically raped by neighboring men.

In such situations, cease-fires are so precarious that some observers have questioned whether—or to what extent—the U.N. should use coercion to establish them. Questions have also been raised about whether it is possible to continue practicing impartiality in the traditional way. Until now, impartiality has meant that U.N. peacekeepers could not act against any of the antagonists, even if they turned belligerent and began violating their own commitments to peaceful conflict resolution. Such restraint will be difficult to justify in the future. But taking

active steps to enforce compliance should not imply that the
U.N. is taking sides in a conflict.[51]

These issues pose a conundrum to the international community, and the key to solving it is to make a clear distinction
between peacekeeping and peacemaking. The peace*keeping*
model was never really meant to apply to situations like those
in which Bosnian women are systematically raped by neighboring men, or in which warlords take possession at gunpoint
of emergency food supplies meant to alleviate starvation in
Somali villages. But the U.N. faces a much greater challenge
now. Without a deliberately-constructed peace*making* or peace
enforcement paradigm—one that establishes guidelines for the
organization's activities and provides adequate resources to carry
them out—there is a considerable danger that the world organization could stumble and fail in its peacemaking attempts.

Collective Security: Making it Work

In the kind of collective security system needed, unlike the ad
hoc one which now exists, priority would be given to enabling
observers to identify potential crises, and to prevent disputes
from escalating into armed conflicts. The United Nations would
be given a greatly strengthened capacity, where conflicts do
erupt, to deal with them through reconciliation efforts, in addition to its traditional peacekeeping activities. It would also
have the power to enforce the terms of cease-fire and peace
agreements. Finally, it would have a capability to help with
establishing conditions that prevent the resumption of violent
conflict at a later stage.

With his June 1992 report to the U.N. Security Council, *An
Agenda for Peace*, Secretary-General Boutros-Ghali seized the initiative for strengthening U.N. peacekeeping and peacemaking.
At the core of his report is a call for member states to make
available, on a standby basis, contingents of their armed forces
for both peacekeeping and cease-fire enforcement purposes.
Boutros-Ghali further emphasizes the importance of preventive
diplomacy. However, the report, as one commentator gently

put it, is "written with an acute sense of the limits of the possible." Boutros-Ghali's ideas make for a good beginning, but they do not provide the framework for a reform of the magnitude required in the long run.[52]

As the U.N.'s capabilities are bolstered, the world community needs to define a set of criteria—in effect create a kind of trigger mechanism—that would activate appropriate elements of this machinery. In addition to breaches of international peace and security, the criteria could include large-scale human rights violations and human suffering induced by warfare. With such a mechanism in place, the danger of the world community standing by idly in the face of such events as the seizing of food by Somali warlords, or the abandonment of Kurdish refugees in Iraq, can be minimized. If a credible mechanism can be established that makes U.N. intervention a virtual certainty under well-defined circumstances, it would likely help to deter at least some acts of aggression and violence.[53]

The successful prevention of conflicts—avoiding the slide toward such levels of savagery and hatred that no peaceful settlement appears even imaginable—requires early and active U.N. involvement. If it is to have any chance of meeting this challenge, it requires a dedicated, competent staff that is large enough to continuously monitor and analyze developments as they unfold around the world, and alert the Secretary-General and Security Council to impending threats to peace and security. A key task would be to prepare what former U.N. official Erskine Childers has called "boundary and ethnic contingency maps"—identifying potential "hot spots" where borders may be contested or contending groups may clash. Early warning alerts would then kick into gear the U.N. machinery for conflict mediation and arbitration.[54]

In view of some of the colossal failures of national intelligence-gathering in the past, it is essential to build some redundancy into early-warning. For example, the Commission on Human Rights might play a role, in conjunction with a (yet to be created) network of regional human rights commissioners. Or, as Boutros-Ghali has suggested, the Economic and Social Council could be utilized to provide reports "on those economic and social developments that may, unless mitigated, threaten international peace and security." The various specialized U.N. agencies already have field offices throughout the world, and could report relevant facts and trends to U.N. headquarters on a regular basis. However, to ensure that bureaucratic layers do not become barriers to action, lines of communication, authority, and responsibility need to be unambiguously established. For example, regional monitoring centers could report directly to a central early-warning office.[55]

Adequate early warning is the keystone of any effort to succeed at defusing and preventing conflicts. Its importance—and its difficulty—can hardly be overstated. Signs of impending violent conflict are not always clearly discernible, and observers may disagree in interpreting the significance of particular developments. Therefore, in addition to maintaining an in-house staff, it would be sensible for the U.N. to contract with outside experts, university departments that specialize in regional affairs, and non-governmental groups such as human rights organizations.

If it is to stay abreast of situations that can change frequently and abruptly, the U.N.'s monitoring capabilities will need to include both individuals in the field and airborne monitoring equipment. Ground-based observers are exposed to the complexities and nuances of evolving situations, able to provide the context and feedback indispensable to any meaningful evaluation of events. But they cannot be omnipresent, and may be prevented from entering certain areas. To complement them, therefore, the U.N. may need to acquire an aerial monitoring capability—a fleet of reconnaissance planes and perhaps even a satellite system.

A satellite capability would provide important information to support preventive diplomacy. By confirming or denying alleged border violations, troop movements, or illicit flows of weapons, or by providing warnings against surprise attacks, it could help build confidence between opposing parties. It could also play a crucial role in monitoring cease-fires, verifying disarmament agreements, and assisting peacekeeping missions. Initially, at least, the U.N. could seek to lease planes and buy commercial satellite time while it assesses its needs and begins to build up its own capacity. Start-up and operating costs of an international satellite monitoring system have been estimated at about $1 billion. The idea was formally introduced in the General Assembly by France in 1978, but has consistently been opposed by the United States and (until the Gorbachev era) the Soviet Union. Without its own satellite system, the U.N. has to rely on the willingness of a handful of governments that possess such monitoring capabilities to share any data. Even if they are prepared to cooperate, the U.N. has no way to ascertain whether the information made available is reliable and unbiased. "We have to be careful because the big powers only give us what they want us to know," laments the U.N.'s Kofi Annan.[56]

At present, the U.N.'s capabilities fall tragically short of needs. In 1987, Secretary-General de Cuéllar set up an Office of Research and the Collection of Information (ORCI) and gave it primary responsibility for early warning. Though it was only a small undertaking, inadequately staffed and funded, it nevertheless had taken five years to persuade the permanent members of the Security Council to agree to its establishment. After another five years, under a reorganization of the U.N. Secretariat in early 1992, ORCI was abolished. Its functions were divided between the Political and Humanitarian Affairs Departments, but no one office has been given true responsibility for early warning. Similarly, a 1988 Soviet proposal to set up "observation posts in explosive areas of the world" was never implemented.[57]

If defiance of U.N. authority occurs without penalty, preventive deployments will quickly lose credibility among both aggressors and those to be protected.

Once an alert of impending conflict is sounded, the U.N. could take actions to diminish the likelihood that violence will actually break out. Where further clarification is needed, fact-finding missions could be dispatched. A unanimously-adopted December 1991 General Assembly declaration empowers not only the Security Council but also the Secretary-General and the Assembly itself to undertake such missions, with the consent of the state onto whose territory a mission is to be sent. So that teams can be dispatched without undue delay, the Assembly recommended that the Secretary-General maintain lists of experts in various fields who could serve on fact-finding missions.[58]

The U.N. can also make fuller use of conflict resolution techniques. Throughout the organization's existence, the Secretaries-General have offered their help in personally mediating disputes—as, for example, they did in the Afghanistan and Iran-Iraq wars. These interventions are often high-profile, last-ditch efforts to avert the outbreak of hostilities, or to halt fighting where it has already begun. But more routine, low-key efforts could help to defuse tensions and resolve disputes at an earlier stage, long before violent conflict is imminent. This function could be served by mechanisms which allow grievances, both within and among nations, to be heard before impartial forums. For instance, David Scheffer of the Carnegie Endowment for International Peace in Washington, D.C. has suggested that the U.N. Trusteeship Council (a body originally charged with decolonization issues) be transformed into a clearinghouse for self-determination issues. Robert Johansen proposes that the Security Council "establish standing conflict resolution committees for each region of the world." The Organization of African Unity is currently studying the establishment of an impartial "ombuds" panel envisaged as a component of the proposed Conference on Security, Stability, Development and Cooperation in Africa.[59]

If an early warning alert or the conclusions of a fact-finding mission warrant it, the U.N. could decide on the preventive deployment of observers or of lightly armed peacekeepers. Monitors could be dispatched to areas where tensions exist but are still sufficiently far from turning violent, while peacekeepers could be sent where violence seems more imminent. For instance, the Security Council recently decided to station a small U.N. observer force in the former Yugoslav republic of Macedonia. The hope is that this gesture will help to prevent the fighting in Bosnia from spilling into Macedonia by focusing

world attention on the region. It may also make sense to consider placing observers in areas of Romania, Slovakia, and
Vojvodina (an autonomous region of Serbia) that are home to
ethnic Hungarians, to help stave off what could develop into
Europe's next major conflict. Likewise, U.N. units could be dispatched to Central Asia, where conflicts in Afghanistan and
Tajikistan threaten to embroil Uzbekistan and perhaps other
countries. Because many more candidates for preventive deployments now exist around the globe, the U.N. needs to develop
guidelines specifying under what circumstances it should become
engaged in this manner, and what additional steps it might
undertake if dispatching observers alone fails to prevent a slide
toward violence.[60]

In *An Agenda for Peace*, Boutros-Ghali proposed that the
Council authorize stationing peacekeepers along international
borders if requested by one or both countries involved in a dispute (with deployments on either one or both sides of the border), or inside countries plagued by internal conflict (though only
with the consent of all parties concerned). The European
Community cautiously endorsed the Secretary-General's proposal in late 1992.[61]

It would be useful to explore the possibilities for vesting
greater authority in the Secretary-General (albeit within clearly-
defined parameters), because the Council may not always be willing or able to act in a timely manner. For example, Robert
Johansen argues that the Secretary-General should be given the
power to send unarmed observers to any international border at
any time, and perhaps to *any* area where heightened tensions
threaten to explode.[62]

The early deployment of a U.N. force could discourage acts
of aggression by symbolizing the international community's
determination to oppose them. However, a determined attack-
er may simply push the peacekeepers aside—as happened in
Lebanon during Israel's 1982 invasion. If such defiance of U.N.
authority occurs without penalty, preventive deployments will
quickly lose credibility among both aggressors and those to be
protected. To be an effective deterrent, a U.N. deployment
would either have to be militarily significant itself (and hence

depart from the peacekeeping model) or be backed up by some other military force—effectively making the peacekeeping force a "tripwire." Since the U.N.'s reputation for fairness rests partly on its past record of restraint, this confronts the organization with a dilemma either way.[63]

Although the U.N. acutely needs a greater preventive capability, the demand for conventional peacekeeping will doubtless continue. It would be unrealistic, of course, to expect the U.N. to be able to stop every future conflict before it turns violent. Moreover, because many of the world's current conflicts are raging without U.N. involvement, the demand for its peacekeeping services could increase if some of those combatants decide to seek an impartial arbiter. Liberia and Nagorno-Karabakh are just two possible candidates. And experience suggests that even many current peacekeeping missions will need to be strengthened if they are not to end in failure—meaning a larger, longer, and more costly U.N. presence than initially envisioned.

The most extensive involvement of U.N. personnel, however, may be required in countries destroyed by years of warfare. In extreme cases, a U.N. "protectorate" or "trusteeship" may be the only viable route to secure the conditions needed for peace-building: the reconstruction both of the physical infrastructure and of a functioning civil society. In effect, this is what the U.N. operations in Cambodia and Somalia are about. Similar intervention may eventually be needed in places like Bosnia, Mozambique, or Angola. Unfortunately, the U.N. is drifting into this role more by default than by deliberation—and as a result may be ill-prepared for the challenges involved. For example, it is likely that over time, any outside entity will come to be perceived as an occupying force.[64]

Reflecting the heightened demand for peacekeeping and peacemaking services since 1988, there is increasing discussion about the merits of a more permanent U.N. force. In *An Agenda for Peace*, Boutros-Ghali recommended that U.N. member states make specially trained contingents of their national armed forces available on a standby basis, an option spelled out in Article 43 of the U.N. Charter but never implemented. He suggested that as many countries as possible make available up to 1,000 troops each on 24 hours' notice for peacekeeping operations. Russia, France, and a number of other European countries support the idea, but the United States, Britain, and China have been either opposed or much less enthusiastic. Governments wanting to respond to Boutros-Ghali's invitation could build on the experience of the Scandinavian countries. Although they do not make troops available automatically (an affirmative decision by each of the national governments involved is required), since 1964 they have had a "Nordic U.N. Standby Force"—a joint system that trains and holds volunteers ready for peacekeeping service.[65]

Following the Article 43 route, however, implies that the troops earmarked for U.N. duty would remain under the direction of their national military establishments until called on by the United Nations. They would thus not assume the separate identity of a U.N. force. And it is not clear that the governments supplying the troops would not retain influence over how these troops are used, compromising the carefully nurtured impartiality of U.N. peacekeeping forces. There is always a danger that U.N. command over national contingents, particularly those from militarily powerful states, is more nominal than real. It is these states that would be disproportionately represented in an on-call U.N. force.[66]

A crucial question is whether U.N. units will continue to be committed to nonviolence.

These problems could be avoided by establishing a permanent peacekeeping force under direct U.N. authority. Unlike an army, it would be neither equipped nor mandated to use force. Its impartiality—and therefore its acceptability—could be emphasized by directly recruiting, from a broad variety of countries, individuals whose loyalty to the U.N. is not in question, rather than forces drawn from sometimes reluctant governments. Establishing a standing force would bring several benefits. Logistical and financial arrangements could be standardized, and the diverse tasks of civilian and military personnel better coordinated. A standing force would also avoid the perennial problem of familiarizing new peacekeepers with U.N. procedures and practices. Peacekeeping units would not be stationed at U.N. headquarters, but instead throughout the world; for example, military bases slated for closure could be made available to them.[67]

Boutros-Ghali has dismissed a permanent peacekeeping force as "impractical and inappropriate," but no detailed study has ever been commissioned to fully explore and scrutinize its political and financial ramifications. However, a permanent force and an on-call force need not be irreconcilable. Initially, the U.N. might set up just a small permanent unit to allow the world's governments to grow accustomed to the idea; before a more sizable permanent force is established, it could draw primarily on standby forces. And even once a larger permanent force is assembled, standby units could still play a backup role wherever needed.[68]

Whether a future U.N. peace force is permanent or standby, its officers will need to have at least some knowledge of the history, politics, culture, and language of the countries and regions they serve in. Even more importantly, they need skills in negotiating and conflict mediating. Systematic training, therefore, is critical. The Scandinavian countries (which together have contributed about one-quarter of all "Blue Helmets" ever dispatched) have established joint programs to train volunteers for peacekeeping missions. Their approach has been emulated by Austria, Malaysia, Poland, and Switzerland. A peacekeeping curriculum is now being introduced at U.S. military academies as well, and a NATO peacekeeping training school is being set up in Germany. But personnel from many other countries have no special peacekeeping expertise.[69]

To assure that it has a sufficient reservoir of competence, the international community would be well advised to set up training programs in each region of the world to impart the many unique non-military skills that successful peacekeeping and peacemaking operations demand. The Norwegian government recently suggested to the U.N. that an international training center be set up in Norway, in conjunction with a proposed national one. Just as governments have set up war academies to study combat tactics and develop new military strategies, the challenge now is to create peace academies, devoted to studying the successes and failures of mediation and negotiation and to devising new methods for peaceful conflict resolution.[70]

A crucial question is whether U.N. units will continue to be committed to nonviolence. U.N. peacekeepers to date have succeeded by adhering to nonviolent principles, thereby encouraging the growth of norms against the use of force. Brian Urquhart, formerly the top U.N. official responsible for peacekeeping and now a scholar at the Ford Foundation, explains that "the principle of nonviolence sets the peacekeeping forces above the conflict they are dealing with: violation of the principle almost invariably leads to the peacekeepers becoming part of the conflict and therefore part of the problem."[71]

The trouble with this ideal is that while the U.N.'s integrity is protected, its authority is increasingly being undermined. In Angola, Cambodia, Western Sahara, and the former Yugoslavia, adversaries that had previously agreed to provisions such as a cease-fire have violated their own commitments with impunity. Peacekeepers face being reduced to marginal importance while indiscriminate fighting inflicts death and misery on innocent civilian populations.

The Bosnian tragedy, in particular, has led to an impassioned debate about the pros and cons of intervention. Most Western governments and the leaders of their militaries have decided that no "strategic" interest is at stake, and therefore have little appetite for getting drawn into what they fear may be a quagmire. But a chorus of commentators has argued for military intervention, denouncing the international community's passivity toward the horror of mass killings, rapes, and "ethnic cleansing." On the other side, however, are those who feel that the use of force does not solve underlying problems, and instead of constraining violence may encourage even more of it. The debate is emblematic of the new uncertainties stirred up by the end of the Cold War. It has deeply divided government officials, policy analysts, and even the peace movement.[72]

Humanity is faced with an anguishing dilemma. Continued reliance on military means—even by the U.N. on behalf of the world community—inevitably re-legitimizes the use of violence for political ends. Those who marvel at the sophistication of modern military technology speak euphemistically of "surgical strikes" directed at aggressors. Realistically, a "just war" still kills and maims not only the perpetrators of barbaric acts but innocent people as well. Yet when the world community stands by, letting innocents be slaughtered, it in effect endorses political change by violent means and sets a dangerous precedent. While it is clearly preferable to prevent situations like the one in Bosnia, the world community has delayed effective nonviolent action there (and in other places) for so long that a strictly peaceful resolution may be no longer possible. In situations where the choice is no longer between violence and no violence, an armed intervention by the international community may be justifiable *if* it will result in the loss of fewer innocent lives than would be the case without such intervention.

If there is to be any use of force by units under U.N. command, can it be clearly differentiated from conventional military actions? Some distinctions can be made with regard to the equipment and mandate involved. A U.N. force should probably not be capable of launching any large-scale offensive operations. Creating an international army designed to outgun any opponent could simply lead national governments or guerrilla movements to become more distrustful—and even more reluctant to disarm. A primarily defensive capacity would allow U.N. forces at least to create safe havens for oppressed groups or for civilians caught in the crossfire. On the other hand, enforcing a cease-fire or disarming recalcitrant fighters would require a more coercive capability.

In view of the events in Bosnia, numerous proposals for a U.N. rapid deployment force or some other military capability have been put forth. In his report to the Security Council, Boutros-Ghali endorses the use of force, by national contingents made available to the U.N., either "to respond to outright aggression, imminent or actual," or to form "peace enforcement units" in cases where a party has agreed to a cease-fire but then goes back on its commitment.[73]

Is there any middle ground between the role of the U.N. as an impartial mediator and that of an assertive peace enforcer that must shed its neutrality and in effect become a warring party? Can the U.N. play both roles, or does one preclude the other?

The answers to these questions, it seems, will emerge less from a detached "grand strategy" discussion than from the organization's day-to-day experience—beginning with Somalia, where the Security Council has empowered U.N. troops to carry out their assigned tasks (disarming warring factions, providing food aid, promoting national reconciliation and reconstruction) with all force necessary. The Somalia operation marks the first time that U.N. peacekeeping forces have been given the mandate for enforcement actions. The next test case may come in Bosnia.[74]

The most sensible solution is to establish a two-tiered U.N. force. The first tier would consist of a permanent, directly recruited and specially trained peacekeeping force that adheres to the principle of nonviolence. The second tier would be composed of more militarily capable standby units, of the kind proposed by Boutros-Ghali, to deter aggression and to enforce cease-fire agreements—if necessary, by disarming and demobilizing warring factions. In most cases, the second tier would function as a backup, mobilized only if peacekeeping units faced severe challenges to their authority. Where an act of aggression seems imminent, it could serve as a first recourse. Such an arrangement would give the U.N. sufficient flexibility to deal adequately with the security challenges of the post-Cold War era.[75]

More than 30 years ago, Adlai Stevenson explained in a speech at the United Nations: "We do not hold the vision of a world without conflict. We do hold the vision of a world without war—and this inevitably requires an alternative system for coping with conflict." Strengthening the U.N.'s capability for preventive diplomacy, peacekeeping, and peacemaking would go a long way toward responding to Stevenson's challenge.[76]

Strengthening the United Nations

The smooth functioning of a machinery for peace depends on the availability of sufficient financial resources. U.N. peacekeeping and peacemaking can be seen as the bargain of the century when their cost is compared with the enormous resources absorbed by the world's larger military machines. Yet

TABLE 4.
Comparison of Military Expenditures and U.N. Peacekeeping Assessments, Selected Countries, 1991

Country	Military Expenditures	Peacekeeping Assessment	Ratio
	(millions of dollars)		
Czechoslovakia	723	3.2	223 : 1
Japan	32,100	55.9	574 : 1
Mexico	662	.9	717 : 1
Germany	39,900	46.0	868 : 1
France	41,400	37.8	1,096 : 1
Nigeria	234	.2	1,191 : 1
Britain	42,300	29.4	1,441 : 1
WORLD	921,500	491.0	1,877 : 1
United States	304,500	151.0	2,016 : 1
China	12,000	4.8	2,520 : 1
Brazil	4,900	1.4	3,441 : 1
Russia	224,100	60.3	3,714 : 1
India	7,200	.4	19,816 : 1
Israel	4,500	.2	21,821 : 1
Pakistan	2,800	.059	47,522 : 1
Syria	4,500	.039	114,562 : 1
Ethiopia	896	.005	182,485 : 1

SOURCE: Adapted from Independent Advisory Group on U.N. Financing, *Financing an Effective United Nations* (New York: Ford Foundation, February 1993).

many member governments fail to pay their fair share for this service. "It's a great irony," Secretary-General Pérez de Cuéllar commented before leaving office in early 1992, "that the U.N. is on the brink of insolvency at the very time the world community has entrusted the organization with new and unprecedented responsibilities." Leaving his post as Under Secretary-General for Administration and Management in early 1993, Richard Thornburgh used more frank language: he compared the financing of peacekeeping operations to a "financial 'bungee jump,' often undertaken in blind faith that timely appropriations will be forthcoming."[77]

U.N. members have accumulated sizable arrears on their dues, both for the regular budget and for peacekeeping missions (most of which are separately assessed). Total unpaid peacekeeping assessments stood at $645 million at the end of 1992—along with unpaid regular dues of $500 million. None of the five permanent Security Council members has paid all it owes, but Russia and the United States are by far the most delinquent. As of December 1992, Russia was $295 million behind and the United States $81 million. Of the 178 member states, only 8 owed no money for peacekeeping. Given this destitute financial situation, the U.N. is forced to scramble for start-up funds every time a new mission is initiated, and is frequently unable to dispatch peacekeepers in a timely manner.[78]

There is no shortage of ideas on how to solidify U.N. finances. Among them are giving the Secretary-General authority to borrow in commercial markets, to charge interest on overdue assessments, or to issue bonds. Perhaps the most obvious potential source is the often bloated military budgets of member nations. In 1991, the world's governments spent $1,877 on their militaries for each $1 they were assessed for U.N. peacekeeping. This average conceals enormous differences among individual countries: for Ethiopia, the ratio was 182,485 to 1, while for Czechoslovakia it was 223 to 1. (See Table 4.) Various proposals have been made—among others, by the Brandt Commission in 1980—to levy a tax on military spending, on the profits of arms manufacturers, or on international arms trade. Without a reliable database, however, this would be impossible. The U.N. arms transfer register, for instance, does not include the monetary value of such transfers. A more useful resource might be the U.N.'s Standardized System of Reporting on Military Expenditure. Although the number of countries that supply the information requested is still small, it has doubled since 1980 to 29, and now includes most of the largest spenders.[79]

Assessing member states for peacekeeping expenses is done on a mission-by-mission basis, frequently conflicting with members' national budget cycles. As an alternative, William Durch and Barry Blechman of the Washington-based Henry Stimson Center have proposed establishing a consolidated annual peace-keeping budget. Boutros-Ghali and his predecessor, Pérez de Cuéllar, have also called for the establishment of a $1-billion peacekeeping endowment to give the U.N. greater financial flex-ibility.[80]

The start-up of a new peacekeeping mission is often the phase most critical to the operation's success, and the expense of purchasing equipment and transporting peacekeepers to their destination also makes this the most costly phase. Yet, on aver-age, as the Independent Advisory Group on U.N. Financing, a panel convened by the Ford Foundation, has noted, only one-third of peacekeeping dues is paid during the first three months of a new mission. To cover start-up expenses, a $150-million start-up fund has recently been authorized, but the Ford Foundation group believes a $400-million fund would be more adequate. In addition, Durch and Blechman have suggested that the Secretary-General be permitted to obligate up to one-third of a new operation's budget as soon as the mission has been authorized by the Security Council (and the approximate bud-get determined), but before the full amount has actually been approved by the General Assembly.[81]

Of course, if the international community were to expand U.N. preventive and peacemaking capabilities in the manner pro-posed here, including the eventual creation of a satellite mon-itoring agency and a related disarmament verification agency, annual expenditures would increase well above today's levels—perhaps to $10 billion or more. But by helping to defuse con-flicts and avert wars, thereby allowing nations to curtail their mil-itary spending, the investment would more than pay for itself.

The conflicts in Central America and the Persian Gulf serve as instructive examples. During the 1980s, the United States spent some $3 billion per year to intervene against the Sandinista government in Nicaragua and revolutionary movements else-where in the region. The Central American countries them-selves spent billions more for military purposes. Between 1980 and 1990, for example, the government of El Salvador spent about $2.5 billion on the war against the FMLN guerrillas, in which some 80,000 people were killed. In negotiations in 1990 and 1991, a peace agreement was reached that gave the U.N. a key role in monitoring human rights and verifying a cease-fire and the separation of forces. At $70 million, the total cost of this U.N. mission since mid-1991 is miniscule compared with the resources expended on the attempted military "solution" to the conflict. The 1991 Persian Gulf war cost about $63 billion. A peacekeeping force large enough to have prevented Iraq's invasion of Kuwait would likely have cost less than one percent of that amount and saved the lives of many thousands of innocent people.[82]

By helping to defuse conflicts and avert wars, the investment in expanded preventive and peacekeeping capabilities would more than pay for itself.

If the U.N. is to move toward a more activist and interventionist stance, it needs not only greater financial backbone but all the political legitimacy it can muster. It is hobbled, however, by the increasingly obsolescent composition of the Security Council—which has "primary responsibility for the maintenance of international peace and security," according to the U.N. Charter, and is the only U.N. body invested with the authority to make decisions that are binding on all member states. Currently, the exclusive club of permanent Council members—with its vaunted veto privileges—consists of the countries that emerged victorious from World War II, and that share the dubious distinction of possessing nuclear weapons and being the world's leading arms exporters: the United States, Russia, China, France, and the United Kingdom. The composition of the Council has become something of an anachronism, since it neither adequately reflects the distribution of power and influence in the world nor constitutes a representative and democratic global body. Large parts of the world, containing two thirds of humanity, have only temporary representation in the Council, in 10 seats rotated among 173 countries.[83]

Throughout the Cold War, the Security Council was deadlocked by the use or threatened use of the veto. Some 242 vetoes were cast between 1946 and 1987. Since then, however, the relationship among the permanent Council members has shifted from confrontation to cooperation, and the Council has been freed from its long paralysis. In the post-Cold War era, the Security Council has become a largely Western-dominated organ: the United States, Britain, and France tend to work in concert; Russia is eager to cement its relationship with the West; and China abstains from voting rather than vetoing resolutions it does not like. Given the new-found consonance within the Council, some observers recommend, "don't fix it if it ain't broke." Yet it is far from clear that the current cooperative spirit will endure. If the Yeltsin government is replaced, for example, Moscow may become less accommodating toward the Western powers. China, too, may decide in the future to use its veto rather than abstain. On the other hand, if the Council is increasingly seen as becoming an instrument of Western policy, rather than an impartial arbiter of conflicts, the U.N. may lose credibility and authority. Boutros-Ghali has warned that "the image will come to be that the United Nations equals the United States, and then many nations will no longer accept the United Nations."[84]

Because of its undemocratic nature, any serious reform of the Council will need to consider the eventual abolition of the veto. Although the permanent five will no doubt resist such a move, the world has changed sufficiently for them to give it serious consideration (China has in the past expressed a willingness to do so). The U.N. framers' intention was that the Security Council have at its disposal military forces adequate to defeat any aggressor, while the veto ensured that no U.N. action would be directed against the permanent five themselves. The Cold War, of course, prevented this form of collective security from becoming reality. Today, even though there is discussion about making standby forces available to the U.N., it seems unlikely that the Council will ever command an army strong enough to challenge any of the permanent five. They could therefore forgo their veto right without fearing for their security.[85]

By virtue of its large population and economic and military

strength, the United States wields enormous influence in international affairs even without anachronistic privileges. In recognition of that fact, the Clinton administration could voluntarily suspend exercising its veto; it could make its suspension contingent on reciprocal action by the other four permanents. Russia and China are less influential than the United States in the global arena, but undoubtedly their voice will be heard in matters important to them even without veto power. It is France and Britain whose prominent Council status is out of sync with their economic, military, and demographic position in today's world. For them, the veto represents one of the last (albeit largely symbolic) vestiges of being a great power; consequently, winning them over is a much more difficult task.[86]

In place of an outright renunciation of the veto, the Security Council members might find it more palatable to relinquish it step-by-step: first with regard to the dispatch of fact-finding missions, then of observer units, and later of lightly-armed peacekeeping forces. Persuading the permanent five to waive their veto privilege with regard to so-called "enforcement" actions will no doubt be more difficult. However, if they perceive that the political benefit

Because of its undemocratic nature, any serious reform of the Council will need to consider the eventual abolition of the veto.

derived from surrendering the veto is likely to outweigh that of clinging to it, relinquishing this outmoded privilege will become more acceptable to them. Also, relinquishing the veto would seem less of a "loss" if the Security Council adopted a weighted voting system instead of one based on straight majorities.[87]

In the current debate about U.N. reform, the idea of expanding the number of permanent seats commands more attention than does the veto issue. Japan and Germany, two of the world's economic superpowers, have expressed a desire to become permanent members. Brazil has proposed that in addition, permanent seats without veto be created for itself and the other largest regional Third World powers—Egypt, India, and Nigeria. It has also been suggested by Italy's former Foreign Minister, Gianni de Michelis, that the French and British seats be merged into a single seat for the European Community. But if Brazil, why not Mexico or Argentina? If Nigeria, why not South Africa? And if India, why not Pakistan or Indonesia? These dilemmas could be avoided by assigning each of the world's regions a permanent (non-veto) seat that would be filled by the leading countries in each region on a rotating basis.[88]

The membership discussion has given rise to a disquieting argument: that if countries like Germany and Japan want to achieve permanent status, they need to be willing to make troops available not only for peacekeeping but also for "enforcement" operations. It is only fair, of course, to demand that all U.N. members share the burden and risks. But if providing troops becomes a requirement for *any* nation to become a permanent Council member, it is tantamount to saying that the willingness to use military force is one of the basic determinants of what makes a nation fit to claim such a seat. Japan and Germany have risen from the ashes of their defeat in World War II by forgoing military means as a legitimate tool of their foreign policies. They could contribute to world peace in non-military ways—for example, by substantially increasing their financial support for the world organization.[89]

The UNA-USA's Jeff Laurenti has suggested that the permanent seats "should not be assigned in perpetuity to named countries but, rather, made subject to periodic renewal based on criteria that might be written into the Charter." Laurenti does not spell out what the criteria for permanent membership ought to be, but in addition to traditional "big power" factors like military and economic muscle, consideration could be given to population size and to financial and other support for the U.N.—perhaps with the stipulation that permanent members jointly represent at least 50 percent of the world total in these categories. And if peaceful conduct is to be given due value, it would be worth considering including at least one country that has been at peace for a long time and shows few signs of militarization.[90]

Even with a reformed Security Council, it may be desirable to give the General Assembly a greater role. According to the U.N. Charter, the Assembly "may discuss any questions relating to the maintenance of international peace and security," but for the most part it has no claws. Deciding on the use of force is the exclusive domain of the Council. And the Assembly is limited to making recommendations, not binding decisions. Richard Hudson, director of the Center for War/Peace Studies in New York, has proposed a "binding triad" that would allow the Assembly to pass binding resolutions on any issue except the use of force, which would remain the prerogative of the Council. The binding triad would consist of a weighted voting system based not only on the current system of one nation, one vote, but also on member countries' population size and their contributions to the regular U.N. budget. For a binding resolution to pass it would need to be approved by a (simple or two-thirds) majority in all three areas. Hudson's concept could be carried further. In addition to initiating action for peaceful conflict resolution, the Assembly might also be given the power to ratify or reject Council decisions in certain critical areas, such as intervention in internal affairs to protect human rights. Approval by the Assembly would bring the full weight of the international consensus to bear, and thus greatly strengthen the legitimacy of any such action. Increasing the Assembly's authority would also reduce the significance of the veto in the Council.[91]

Establishing the U.N. is the closest the world community has ever come to creating a global parliament. Yet the U.N. is still composed of representatives of national governments with vastly different degrees of legitimacy. A popularly-elected "world citizens assembly," perhaps constituted as a second chamber alongside the existing General Assembly, would inject greater grassroots input, and accountability, into deliberations that concern the future of world peace and justice. Voting in a second chamber could also be structured according to the binding triad concept.[92]

Clearly, any reforms as fundamental as those suggested here are unlikely to materialize soon unless people in all societies mobilize on their behalf. Amending the U.N. Charter requires a two-thirds majority in the General Assembly and the backing of all five permanent Security Council members. No doubt, one or more of the "veto powers" will be loath to relinquish their special status. In any dilution of their strength, there is a trade-off. If the big powers feel too constrained by the U.N., they might be tempted to act unilaterally. But as the Iraq-Kuwait crisis has shown, even militarily powerful states seek the mantle of legitimacy that the U.N. confers—they want to use the U.N. when it serves their interest. If enough countries feel that only a more representative Security Council can legitimately exercise its mandate to maintain international peace and security, the big powers will be compelled to allow some change.

Conclusion

The momentum of human conflict in the 1990s is such that for the world's governments, the task of maintaining peace and security cannot simply be carried on in the future—each nation fending for itself—as it has been in the past. Either a new mechanism of collective security will be firmly established and financed, or nations will find themselves increasingly embattled—and fractured—by challenges to their economic viability, cultural integrity, and sovereignty.

The question facing the international community now is whether a strengthened U.N. peacekeeping system can offer a workable and affordable alternative to the use of force by national governments and their adversaries. The answer can be found in the two types of conflict the U.N. now faces—and that any successful security system will have to cope with: transborder attacks like Iraq's 1991 invasion of Kuwait, and civil wars like that now raging in the former Yugoslavia.

In the first case, there is good reason to conclude that the conflict would have taken a different course had the U.N.'s capabilities already been strengthened as proposed here. Iraq's invasion was preceded by clear signs of a gathering storm. Greater attention to preventive diplomacy would not have ignored the Iraq-Kuwait dispute over oil production and prices that was a key factor leading up to the assault. Once Iraqi troops began assembling near the border, the U.N. could have quickly dispatched a peacekeeping force. While not a militarily significant counterweight, it would have underscored the international community's determination to prevent the takeover of Kuwait. Backup forces could have been mobilized by the U.N. to demonstrate the world's firmness. In any event, had Iraq's military buildup during the 1980s not been so eagerly assisted by many governments and private companies, and its genocide against the Kurds so ignored, it would not have required a massive show of force to dissuade Baghdad from invading Kuwait.

In the former Yugoslavia, too, the slide toward violence was quite predictable. As Sabrina Petra Ramet, an associate professor of international studies at the University of Washington, notes, "by 1987 ordinary Yugoslavs were talking openly about the growing danger of civil war." A series of local elections held in 1990 resulted in majorities for narrowly-based ethnic parties. It is clear now that this was a missed last opportunity for the international community to become involved, by offering assistance to accomplish the breakup of Yugoslavia peacefully. The U.S. and Western European governments at first urged Yugoslav unity (seen by Serbia as a green light to hold the federation together by force), then abruptly recognized Slovenia and Croatia as independent states, before sufficient rights and protections for minorities were established—in effect giving Serbs an excuse to commence violence. It became clear that the pattern of violence could be repeated in Bosnia, yet the European Community endorsed "cantonization," in effect encouraging the "ethnic cleansing" by Bosnian Serbs that followed. Any last hope of dissuasion by the U.N. was extinguished when the Security Council discussed, but did not send, a proposed large peacekeeping force prior to the outbreak of hostilities.[93]

It is always easier in hindsight to determine what actions might have been taken to avoid undesired outcomes. As a result, it is only realistic to assume that some opportunities for peaceful conflict resolution will continue to be missed in the future, that diplomacy will not always be as effective as it could be, and that the antagonists may prefer to fight rather than negotiate. The international community will need to learn—by trial and error, at first—how to employ the tools of preventive diplomacy and peacemaking effectively. The U.N.'s current, large-scale peacemaking efforts in Cambodia, Somalia, and the former Yugoslavia could turn out to be crucial tests—watershed events in the long history of human conflict. If these operations go seriously awry, the world community's willingness to vest greater authority in the U.N. may quickly fade.

Can sufficient political will be marshaled to revamp the U.N. enough to make it undeniably effective? Governments may not be keen to invest in peacemaking aimed at seemingly remote conflicts where none of their interests seem to be directly at stake. They may still be reluctant to get directly involved *themselves*, even when the fighting is geographically nearby. In that case, however, they will almost certainly be more anxious to devise a collective security mechanism for coping with violent conflict.

Between the end of World War II and the beginning of the 1990s, Europeans and Americans grew accustomed to the facile notion that wars and civil strife are confined to faraway lands. Perhaps the only "silver lining" that can be detected in the horrible events in the former Yugoslavia is that they jolted Europeans to realize that their region is not immune to violent conflicts—and that complacency at home is not a viable response to human violence abroad. Officials may still prefer to simply contain the Balkans conflict or, to the extent possible, ignore it. But if the international community does not equip the U.N. so that it can deal with *any* conflicts, however remote, it will be unprepared for those cases in which a majority of governments do perceive a need for a collective security approach. Letting acts of blatant violence occur sets a precedent of sorts, increasing the likelihood that they will be repeated elsewhere. If the world's governments (and particularly those controlling the U.N.'s funding) recognize that in an interconnected world, security and human rights are ultimately indivisible, they will be more willing to create an effective machinery for peace.

Even while fundamental issues concerning the shape of a future collective security system remain unresolved, some steps can be taken immediately because they are neither controversial nor costly. These include setting up pools of experienced military observers, fact-finding personnel, and human rights monitors on which the U.N. could draw on short notice; taking measures now to ensure that by 1995 (the organization's 50th anniversary) the U.N. will have a functioning early-warning office; and empowering the Secretary-General to start recruiting and training individuals for a pilot permanent peacekeeping unit, which over time could become the core of a more sizable force. Finally, the upcoming anniversary presents a good target date by which members could resolve to finish paying off their outstanding dues and to establish a regular peacekeeping and peacemaking fund.[94]

Mobilizing sufficient support for more far-reaching reforms, including any requiring Charter amendments, will clearly take more time. But the very invention of peacekeeping—an activity not provided for in the U.N. Charter—suggests that the world organization's founding document is flexible enough to accommodate creative new approaches to making peace, even short of charter revision.

The perception that national interests collide with a strengthened United Nations may still preclude rapid reform. Yet in region after region, the dangers of reverting to violence as a means of settling differences are becoming clear. The aftermath of destructive and exhaustive wars that fail to achieve combatants' original objectives proves the point. The question is whether the nations of the world are prepared to transform the United Nations from a peacekeeper of last resort to a peacemaker of first, and routine, recourse.

That human history is riddled, and even largely defined, by patterns of violent conflict leads many people to assume that war is part of human nature and is therefore unavoidable. Yet, at the same time that humans have strived to perfect technologies of destruction, they have also struggled to define acceptable behavior during war and—more recently, and haltingly, but with growing confidence—to establish norms against the use of violence. Just because war is a social institution does not mean it is inevitable: created by us, it can also be abolished by us.

Notes

1. William Eckhardt, "War-Related Deaths Since 3000 BC," *Bulletin of Peace Proposals*, Vol. 22, No. 4 (1991); Melvin Small and J. David Singer, "Patterns in International Warfare, 1816-1965," in Richard A. Falk and Samuel S. Kim (eds.), *The War System: An Interdisciplinary Approach* (Boulder, Colo.: Westview Press, 1980).

2. Edwin Chen, "For Troops at Border 'It's Kickoff Time'," *Los Angeles Times*, Feb. 25, 1991.

3. Benjamin R. Barber, "Jihad Vs. McWorld," *The Atlantic Monthly*, March 1992.

4. Robert C. Johansen, "The Reagan Administration and the U.N.: The Costs of Unilateralism," *World Policy Journal*, Fall 1986.

5. The conflicts that share some characteristics of inter-state war include the following: the dispute between Armenia and Azerbaijan over the status of Nagorno-Karabakh; the Kashmir conflict involving India and Pakistan; the fighting in the former Yugoslavia; and the Israeli-Palestinian conflict. Map 1 is assembled on the basis of the following sources: Birger Heldt, Peter Wallensteen, and Kjell-Åke Nordquist, "Major Armed Conflicts in 1991," in Stockholm International Peace Research Institute (SIPRI), *SIPRI Yearbook 1992: World Armaments and Disarmament* (Oxford: Oxford University Press, 1992); Center for Defense Information (CDI), "World at War—1992," *The Defense Monitor*, Vol. 21, No. 6 (1992); Ernie Regehr, "A World Made Safe for War?," *Ploughshares Monitor*, December 1992; and David Binder with Barbara Crossette, "As Ethnic Wars Multiply, U.S. Strives for a Policy," *New York Times*, February 7, 1993.

6. Ruth Leger Sivard, *World Military and Social Expenditures 1989* (Washington, D.C.: World Priorities, 1989); Ernie Regehr, "A Pattern of War," *Ploughshares Monitor*, December 1991.

7. Quindlen argues: "If husbands are never able to embrace again wives whom they know to have been violated, if women so violated recoil from sexual contact, if families reject daughters twice victimized, by violence and then by the strictures of a culture that esteems virginity—then it is possible that the rape policy will help wipe out the Bosnian Muslims." Anna Quindlen, "Gynocide," *New York Times*, March 10, 1993.

8. Refugees from Hal Kane, "Refugees Reach All-Time Record," in Lester R. Brown, Ed Ayres, and Hal Kane, *Vital Signs 1993* (New York: W.W. Norton & Co., 1993, forthcoming), and from Hal Kane, "A Deluge of Refugees," *World Watch*, November/December 1992.

9. Heldt et al., op. cit., note 5; CDI, op. cit., note 5. For example, an estimated 200,000 people are estimated to have been killed in East Timor, equal to one-third of the entire population.

10. Generally, for analytical purposes conflicts are considered major if they have killed at least 1,000 persons.

11. Afghanistan in top five of arms recipients from Ian Anthony, et al., "The Trade in Major Conventional Weapons," in SIPRI, op. cit., note 5.

12. Erskine Childers, "UN Mechanisms and Capacities for Intervention," in Elizabeth G. Ferris (ed.), *The Challenge to Intervene: A New Role for the United Nations?*, Conference Report 2 (Uppsala, Sweden: Life and Peace Institute, 1992). Regehr, op. cit., note 5. For the link between environmental and resource issues and violent conflict, see Thomas Homer-Dixon, "On the Threshold: Environmental Changes as Causes of Acute Conflict," *International Security*, Fall 1991, and Thomas Homer-Dixon, Jeffrey H. Boutwell, and George W. Rathjens, "Environmental Change and Violent Conflict," *Scientific American*, February 1993.

13. Balkans from Charles Gati, "From Sarajevo to Sarajevo," *Foreign Affairs*, Fall 1992, and from Kristian Gerner, "From the Black Sea to the Adriatic: Ethnicity, Territory and International Security," *Security Dialogue*, March 1993. Ted Robert Gurr, "Third World Minorities at Risk Since 1945," Background Paper on the Conference on Conflict Resolution in the Post-Cold War Third World, U.S. Institute of Peace, Washington, D.C., October 3-5, 1990.

14. See Charles William Maynes, "Containing Ethnic Conflict," *Foreign Policy*, Spring 1993, for more discussion.

15. Map 2 is adapted from Ante Markotic, Ejub Sijerac, and Asim Abdurahmanovic, "Bosnia-Herzegovina 1991: The Ethnic Makeup of the Republic," *War Report*, November/December 1992. Vesna Pesic, a delegate to the grassroots-organized Conference for a Balkan Peace meeting in September 1992, argued: "If we recognize changes of borders, then war will never stop—in fact it will spread." See "Conference for a Balkan Peace," *War Report*, September 1992.

16. For additional discussion, see Maynes, op. cit., note 14, and "Nationalism and Ethnic Particularism," *Tikkun*, November/December 1992. Lebanon from *MERIP Reports*, October 1983, Issue on "Lebanon in Crisis."

17. Zoran Pajic, "Salvaging the Bosnian Ideal," *War Report*, October 1992.

18. Conflict Resolution Program, The Carter Center, as reported in "Carnage Unseen," *New York Times*, April 11, 1993. Trend of major and "lesser" wars from "Anzahl der pro Jahr geführten und der neu begonnenen Kriege," *Frieden 2000*, February 1993.

19. Cumulative world military spending from Michael Renner, "Military Expenditures Falling," in Lester R. Brown, Christopher Flavin, and Hal Kane, *Vital Signs 1992* (New York: W.W. Norton & Co., 1992). 1992 weapons quantities compiled from International Institute for Strategic Studies, *The Military Balance 1992-1993* (London: Brassey's, 1992). Major surface warships include aircraft carriers, cruisers, destroyers, and frigates. Cumulative arms transfers calculated from Arms Control and Disarmament Agency (ACDA), *World Military Expenditures and Arms Transfers* (Washington, D.C.: U.S. Government Printing Office, various editions). For Third World countries with significant arms production, see Ian Anthony, "The 'Third Tier' Countries: Production of Major Weapons," in Herbert Wulf (ed.), *Arms Industry Limited* (Oxford: SIPRI/Oxford University Press, 1993).

20. The pitfalls of the balance-of-power approach are discussed by Robert C. Johansen, *Toward an Alternative Security System*, World Policy Paper No. 24 (New York: World Policy Institute, 1983).

21. For further discussion, see Robert C. Johansen, "Do Preparations for War Increase or Decrease International Security?," in Charles W. Kegley, Jr. (ed.), *The Long Postwar Peace. Contending Explanations and Projections* (New York: Harper Collins, 1991). In a study for the Overseas Development Council in Washington, D.C., Nicole Ball argues that military aid has enabled some Third World countries to maintain much larger military forces than would have been possible without such assistance. It has allowed many countries to engage in warfare and to avoid seeking compromises with their opponents. Nicole Ball, *Pressing for Peace: Can Aid Induce Reform?*, Policy Essay No. 6 (Washington, D.C.: Overseas Development Council, 1992).

22. Jeffrey Clark, "Debacle in Somalia," *Foreign Affairs*, America and the World 1992/93 issue.

23. Table 1 is a Worldwatch compilation based on Serge Sur (ed.), *Verification of Current Disarmament and Arms Limitation Agreements: Ways, Means and Practices* (Aldershot, UK: Dartmouth Publishing Co., 1991), on SIPRI, op. cit., note 5, on Institute for Defense and Disarmament Studies (IDDS), *The Arms Control Reporter 1992* (Cambridge, Mass.: 1992), and on ACDA, "Treaty Between the United States of America and the Russian Federation on Further Reduction and Limitation of Strategic Offensive Arms," Official Text, Office of Public Affairs, Washington, D.C., January 3, 1993.

24. Whereas the Nuclear Non-Proliferation Treaty represents a multilateral bargain that, on paper at least, commits the nuclear powers to disarmament efforts, nonproliferation measures in other fields, such as the 1987 Missile Technology Control Regime or the so-called Australia Group (chemical and biological agents), are no more than unilaterally imposed export controls by a cartel of western supplier nations. Andrew Mack, "Missile Proliferation, Proliferation Control and the Question of Transparency," in United Nations Department for Disarmament Affairs (UNDDA), *Transparency in International Arms Transfers*, Disarmament Topical Paper 3 (New York: United Nations, 1990); "The Techies vs. the Techno-Cops," *Business Week*, June 15, 1992. Dual-use issue from Greg Bischak and James Raffel, "Economic Conversion and International Inspection: Alternatives to Arms Exports and Militarism," presented at the International Working Conference on the Arms Trade, New York, October 31-November 2, 1991.

25. Michael Renner, "Preparing for Peace," in Lester R. Brown et al., *State of the World 1993* (New York: W.W. Norton & Co., 1993).

26. CDI, "Nuclear Weapons After the Cold War: Too Many, Too Costly, Too Dangerous," *The Defense Monitor*, Vol. 22, No. 1 (1993); Richard Fieldhouse et al., "Nuclear Weapon Developments and Unilateral Reduction Initiatives," in SIPRI, op. cit., note 5; Michael Renner, "Finishing the Job," *World Watch*, November/December 1992. One nation that was long thought to clandestinely have developed nuclear arms was South Africa. President de Klerk recently confirmed the suspicion but said all devices had been destroyed again. Bill Keller, "South Africa Says It Built 6 Atom Bombs," *New York Times*, March 25, 1993.

27. IDDS, op. cit., note 23; Thomas Bernauer, "The End of Chemical Warfare," *Security Dialogue*, March 1993; Amy E. Smithson, "Chemical Weapons: The End of the Beginning," *Bulletin of the Atomic Scientists*, October 1992. A large number of countries has signed the convention; holdouts include a number of Arab countries (that make Israel's accession to the Nuclear Non-Proliferation Treaty a precondition for signing), North Korea, and Vietnam. William Drozdiak, "Historic Treaty Bans Chemical Weapons," *Washington Post*, January 14, 1993. Jozef Goldblat and Thomas Bernauer, "Towards a More Effective Ban on Biological Weapons," *Bulletin of Peace Proposals*, Vol. 23, No. 1 (1992).

28. Jane M.O. Sharp, "Conventional Arms Control in Europe," in SIPRI, *SIPRI Yearbook 1991* (Oxford: Oxford University Press, 1991); IDDS, op. cit., note 23 (1990, 1991, and 1992 editions). In a sense, the CFE Treaty simply codifies measures that, at the time of its signature, had already been undertaken or announced by members of the now-defunct Warsaw Treaty Organization. See Ian Anthony et al., *West European Arms Production* (Stockholm: SIPRI, 1990).

29. Arms trade statistic from Anthony et al., op. cit., note 11.

30. Herbert Wulf, "Recent Trends in Arms Transfers and Possible Multilateral Action for Control," and Alessandro Corradini, "Consideration of the Question of International Arms Transfers by the United Nations," both in UNDDA, op. cit., note 24. Even as the Cold War came to an end, U.S. arms sales abroad nearly quadrupled between 1987 and 1992. See Eric Schmitt, "Arms Makers' Latest Tune: 'Over There, Over There,'" *New York Times*, October 4, 1992.

31. Lack of attempts to restrain arms transfers from Susan Willett, *Controlling the Arms Trade: Supply and Demand Dynamics*, Faraday Discussion Paper No. 18, The Council for Arms Control, University of London, November 1991. Talks among largest exporters from Anthony et al., op. cit., note 11, especially Appendix 8A, and from Natalie J. Goldring, "Arms Trade Talks Future in Doubt," *BASIC Reports*, September 21, 1992.

32. In 1974, eight Latin American countries signed the Ayacucho Declaration, which was intended to negotiate regional limitations on arms imports and on military expenditures. But the declaration was never implemented. Wulf, op. cit., note 30; Michael Brzoska, "The Nature and Dimension of the Problem," in UNDDA, op. cit., note 24.

33. The text of the arms register resolution can be found in U.N. General Assembly, "Transparency in Armaments," A/RES/46/36, 66th Plenary Meeting, New York, December 9, 1991. Quote is from Anthony et al., op. cit., note 11.

34. Anthony et al., op. cit., note 11; "Natalie J. Goldring, "UN Arms Register Takes Shape," *BASIC Reports*, August 17, 1992; for a private-group effort to draft a treaty on a mandatory arms register and a comprehensive program for the eventual elimination of arms transfers, see "Draft Convention on the Monitoring, Reduction, and Ultimate Abolition of the International Arms Trade," *Alternatives. Social Transformation and Humane Governance*, Winter 1992.

35. Sur (ed.), op. cit., note 23; Patricia Lewis, *Verification and Disarmament* (London: Scientists Against Nuclear Arms, 1991); Patricia M. Lewis, "The Conventional Forces in Europe Treaty," in J.B. Poole, (ed.), *Verification Report 1991. Yearbook on Arms Control and Environmental Agreements* (New York: Apex Press, 1991).

36. Ibid.; Regina Cowen Karp, "The START Treaty and the Future of Strategic Nuclear Arms Control," Appendix 1A: Excerpts from the 1991 START Treaty and

Related Documents, in SIPRI, op. cit., note 5; ACDA, op. cit., note 23; Jay Brin, "Ending the Scourge of Chemical Weapons," *Technology Review*, April 1993. ACDA director Ronald Lehman called the Chemical Weapons Convention the "most intrusive inspection regime ever established in an arms control agreement." Quoted in David White, "The World Tries to End Horror of Poison Gas," *Financial Times*, January 13, 1993.

37. The Chemical Weapons Convention is the only arms treaty that sets up an independent, multilateral verification agency—the Organization for the Prohibition of Chemical Weapons in The Hague; all other agreements are verified on a national or military alliance level. The Convention establishes an elaborate institutional structure, including a Scientific Advisory Board, review conferences in five-year intervals, an Executive Council, and a Technical Secretariat to conduct inspections. It is planned that the Secretariat will have a staff of up to 1,000 and an annual budget of $150-180 million. IDDS, op. cit., note 23; Frances Williams, "Hopes High for International Chemical Weapons Treaty," *Financial Times*, August 26, 1992. For more discussion of the merits of a verification agency, see Aram Fuchs, "The Potential for a UN Verification Agency," in Walter Hoffmann (ed.), *A New World Order: Can it Bring Security to the World's People?* (Washington, D.C.: World Federalist Association, September 1991).

38. De Cuéllar quoted in Paul Lewis, "U.N. Chief Warns of Costs of Peace," *New York Times*, December 11, 1988.

39. Jeffrey Laurenti, *The Common Defense: Peace and Security in a Changing World* (New York: United Nations Association of the United States (UNA-USA), 1992). Peacekeeping operations are authorized by the Security Council and their funding approved by the General Assembly. The Secretary-General is in charge of day-to-day operations, with a commanding general who has been approved by the Council.

40. Prior to 1991, the largest U.N. operation took place in the former Republic of Congo (now Zaire) in 1960-1964, involving up to 19,825 people. Brief descriptions of all peacekeeping operations up to 1989 can be found in Joseph Preston Baratta, *International Peacekeeping: History and Strengthening*, Monograph No. 6 (Washington, D.C.: The Center for U.N. Reform Education, November 1989); more recent ones are described in United Nations Department of Public Information (UNDPI), "United Nations Peace-Keeping Operations: Information Notes," New York, September 1992. In addition to these two publications, Table 2 is based on William J. Durch and Barry M. Blechman, *Keeping the Peace: The United Nations in the Emerging World Order* (Washington, D.C.: The Henry L. Stimson Center, 1992), on Marjorie Ann Brown, "United Nations Peacekeeping: Historical Overview and Current Issues," *CRS Report for Congress*, Congressional Research Service, Washington, D.C., January 31, 1990, on UNDPI, "Background Note: United Nations Peace-Keeping Operations," PS/DPI/15/Rev.3, January 1993, on UNDPI, various private communications, and on Michael Littlejohns, "Peace Cost Put at $1.55 bn," *Financial Times*, March 16, 1993.

41. Cumulative number of peacekeepers from UNDPI, "Background Note," op. cit., note 40; cumulative spending from Boutros Boutros-Ghali, *An Agenda for Peace: Preventive Diplomacy, Peacemaking and Peacekeeping*, Report of the Secretary-General Pursuant to the Statement Adopted by the Summit Meeting of the

Security Council on January 31, 1992 (New York: United Nations, 1992). 1987 peacekeeping spending from William Branigin, "Missteps on the Path to Peace," *Washington Post*, September 22, 1992; 1992 spending from Independent Advisory Group on U.N. Financing, *Financing an Effective United Nations* (New York: Ford Foundation, February 1993). Air Force purchase from Department of Defense, *Program Acquisition Costs by Weapon System. Department of Defense Budget for Fiscal Year 1993* (Washington, D.C.: National Technical Information Service, January 29, 1992). Cost estimate for Somalia operation from Littlejohns, op. cit., note 40. Costs of Bosnia enforcement operation from Paul Lewis, "U.N. Is Developing Control Center to Coordinate Growing Peacekeeping Role," *New York Times*, March 28, 1993. 1990 strength of peacekeepers from Lewis, op. cit., note 38; growth toward 100,000 based on Leslie Crawford, "UN to Enter Uncharted Territory," *Financial Times*, March 16, 1993; possible deployments in Bosnia from Michael R. Gordon, "U.S. Is Urging Nato to Prepare Force for Duty in Bosnia," *New York Times*, March 11, 1993.

42. Lewis, op. cit., note 41. 1992 staff from Edward Mortimer, "A Victim of Its Own Success," *Financial Times*, January 22, 1993.

43. Table 3 is a Worldwatch compilation, based primarily on the following sources: Cyprus: Claas Möller, "Kein Kompromiß in Sicht," *Der Überblick*, September 1992; Frank J. Prial, "U.N. Report Sees Hope on Cyprus," *New York Times*, August 26, 1992. Angola: Michael Holman, "UN Struggles to Avert Angola Nightmare," *Financial Times*, January 15, 1993; Paul Lewis, "U.N. Chief Threatens to Pull Troops Out of Angola," *New York Times*, January 27, 1993; Kenneth B. Noble, "A New Crisis Engulfs Angola as the Rebels Make Big Gains," *New York Times*, January 29, 1993; Marrack Goulding, "U.N. Can't Force Peace on Parties in Angola" (letter to the editor), *New York Times*, March 1, 1993. Western Sahara: Waltraud Schütz, "Unfaire Vermittler?," *Der Überblick*, September 1992. Cambodia: Susanne Feske and Christopher Daase, "Ehrgeiziger Fahrplan," *Der Überblick*, September 1992; Victor Mallet, "UN Soldiers Fail to Pacify the Killing Fields," *Financial Times*, February 11, 1993; William Branigin, "U.N. Officials Say Cambodian Election at Risk," *Washington Post*, February 15, 1993; Henry Kamm, "Cambodia Election Snared as Peace Pact Unravels," *New York Times*, March 18, 1993. Croatia: John Darnton, "Croats and Serbs Broaden Battle; U.N. Pessimistic," *New York Times*, January 28, 1993; Phillip Schwarm, "Singing the Blues: Armed Hostage in the Balkans," *War Report*, January 1993. Bosnia: Vanessa Vasic Janekovic and Anthony Borden, "Bosnia-Herzegovina: National Parties and the Plans for Division," *War Report*, November/December 1992; "A Diary of Disgrace," *New York Times*, December 20, 1992; U.N. Security Council, "Report of the Secretary-General on the Activities of the International Conference on the Former Yugoslavia," S/25221, New York, February 2, 1993; Gordon, op. cit., note 41. Somalia: Jane Perlez, "No Easy Fix for Somalia," *New York Times*, September 7, 1992; Rakiya Omaar, "Alptraum ohne Ende," *Der Überblick*, September 1992; Eric Schmitt, "Most U.S. Troops Will Leave Somalia by April in U.N. Plan," *New York Times*, February 13, 1993; Paul Lewis, "U.N. Will Increase Troops in Somalia," *New York Times*, March 27, 1993; "Pact on Somalia Reported by U.N.," *New York Times*, March 28, 1993.

44. The support provided by some governments, including those of Canada and the Scandinavian countries, has been exemplary. But other governments' reservations toward U.N. peacekeeping are illustrated most recently in Mozambique and Bosnia. The U.N. Security Council has approved a force of about 7,500 peacekeepers for Mozambique, but the U.N. has had difficulty finding enough member governments willing to contribute troops. The dispatch of the force has fallen far behind schedule. See Bill Keller, "Mozambique's Outlook Brightens as Truce Holds and Drought Ends," *New York Times*, February 22, 1993. In Bosnia, the United Kingdom and France, both of which have sent soldiers for peace-keeping duty, "insist on more control over operations than is customary in U.N. peacekeeping operations." Hella Pick, "Knee-Deep in the Imbroglio," *The Guardian*, September 11, 1992. Financial uncertainties and other difficulties almost derailed the U.N.'s mission in Namibia, and delayed U.N. involvement in Somalia, Cambodia, Croatia, and Bosnia. See Edward C. Luck, "Making Peace," *Foreign Policy*, Winter 1992/1993, and Enid C.B. Schoettle, "U.N. Dues: The Price of Peace," *Bulletin of the Atomic Scientists*, June 1992.

45. Television has brought pressure on governments to not just stand by and watch the violent disintegration of societies. But TV coverage is uneven (focus-ing on one or a few cases while disregarding others) and oriented toward spec-tacular events (while neglecting less sensational developments that may be equally severe in their implications for human life); furthermore, TV audiences tend to grow tired of being fed the same pictures evening after evening and may lose interest. Television therefore is an unreliable trigger for action.

46. Roberta Cohen, "UN Human Rights Bodies: An Agenda for Humanitarian Action," in Ferris (ed.), op. cit., note 12. For further discussion, see, Elizabeth Ferris, "Intervention, Sovereignty, and the United Nations," Wil D. Verwey, "Legality of Humanitarian Intervention after the Cold War," and Ninan Koshy, "Morality and International Law: An Ethic of Intervention?," all in Ferris (ed.), op. cit., note 12; further, David J. Scheffer, Richard N. Gardner, and Gerald B. Helman, *Three Views on the Issue of Humanitarian Intervention* (Washington, D.C.: U.S. Institute of Peace, 1992), and Indar Jit Rikhye, *Strengthening UN Peacekeeping: New Challenges and Proposals* (Washington, D.C.: U.S. Institute of Peace, 1992).

47. Abdullahi Ahmed An-Na'im, "Third World Perspectives," in Ferris (ed.), op. cit., note 12.

48. Santiago Declaration from Winrich Kühne, "Blauhelme in einer Turbulenten Welt," *Der Überblick*, September 1992. Boutros Boutros-Ghali, "Empowering the United Nations," *Foreign Affairs*, Winter 1992/1993.

49. Elizabeth Harris, research director of the Life and Peace Institute in Uppsala, Sweden, has commented that "the human rights violations of the government of Iraq, which had been ignored for years, became a way of mobilizing support for the political interests of a small group of Western governments" after Saddam Hussein's invasion of Kuwait. "The selective intervention on behalf of Kurdish refugees as a result of the Gulf War did not apply to Kurds elsewhere." The United States and its allies set up a safe zone for Kurds in northern Iraq, but did nothing to protect Kurds in Turkey, a key U.S. ally. Elizabeth Ferris, "An Overview of the Issues," in Ferris (ed.), op. cit., note 12. For Sudan, see John Prendergast, "Helping Sudanese End their Civil War," *Christian Science Monitor*, March 15, 1993.

50. Edward C. Luck and Tobi Trister Gati, "Whose Collective Security?" *The Washington Quarterly*, Spring 1992.

51. The dispatch of a large U.N. peacekeeping force to Somalia marks the first time that the U.N. has intervened without a specific host country request. There, the U.N. will soon also be confronted with the issue of use of force; the Security Council has already approved the use of force to ensure delivery of food and medicine (Council Resolution 794, passed in 1992). See Schmitt, op. cit., note 43.

52. Boutros-Ghali, op. cit., note 41; Mark Sommer, "A UN With Teeth," *Christian Science Monitor*, December 14, 1992.

53. Larry Minear has suggested areas in which criteria could be developed to determine whether any U.N. intervention should take place. They include the number of persons affected, the severity of the threat to human life, the generation of substantial flows of refugees, and the demonstrated inability of the government to cope with the magnitude of the crisis. Larry Minear, testimony before the House Select Committee on Hunger, U.S. Congress, July 30, 1991, as cited in Ferris, op. cit., note 49. Childers, op. cit., note 12.

54. Contingency mapping from Childers, op. cit., note 12.

55. The U.N. human rights system, particularly concerning enforcement, is still very weak. See Cohen, op. cit., note 46. Boutros-Ghali, op. cit., note 41. The Economic and Social Council per se is too large a body for an effective early warning function; it might, however, create a special subsidiary body for this purpose. The U.N. Development Program has 115 offices around the world, and there are 67 U.N. information offices. See Walter Hoffmann (ed.), *Rethinking Basic Assumptions About the United Nations*, Conference Report (Washington, D.C.: World Federalist Association, February 1993).

56. Cost estimate cited by Daniel Deudney, "The High Frontier of Outer Space in the 1990s: Star Wars or Spaceship Earth?" in Michael T. Klare and Daniel C. Thomas (eds.), *World Security: Trends and Challenges at Century's End* (New York: St. Martin's Press, 1991). The U.N. could buy time on the French or Russian satellite surveillance system, which is available on a commercial basis. See the suggestion by Charles William Maynes, "Between Inertia and the 82nd Airborne," *Washington Post*, October 25, 1992. The U.N. is now trying to receive military surveillance information from the United States and any other country willing to share such information. The U.S. government is planning to make available to the U.N., on a commercial basis, satellite pictures for the Somalia peacekeeping operation. Satellite information and Annan quote from Lewis, op. cit., note 41.

57. Paul Lewis, "Soviets Say U.N. Peacekeeping Effort Should Emphasize Prevention," *New York Times*, October 18, 1988. ORCI from "A U.N. Office Looks to Prevent War," *New York Times*, April 16, 1989; Jürgen Dedring, "Konfliktverhütung," *Der Überblick*, September 1992.

58. U.N. General Assembly, "Declaration on Fact-Finding by the United Nations in the Field of the Maintenance of International Peace and Security," Resolution 46/59, adopted December 9, 1991, as reprinted in UNDPI, *Resolutions and*

Decisions Adopted by the General Assembly During the First Part of its 46th Session (New York, January 21, 1992). Walter Dorn, "Keeping Watch for Peace: Fact-Finding by the UN Secretary-General," unpublished paper, Parliamentarians for Global Action, New York, October 1992. Secretary-General Boutros-Ghali has sent missions to Moldavia, Georgia, Armenia, Azerbaijan, and Tajikistan since the passage of the Assembly resolution. See Dedring, op. cit., note 57.

59. Scheffer's proposal from Lucia Mouat, "Broad Mission, Small Budget Strain UN Effort," *Christian Science Monitor*, July 27, 1992. Robert C. Johansen, "Lessons for Collective Security," *World Policy Journal*, Summer 1991; Robert C. Johansen, "UN Peacekeeping: The Changing Utility of Military Force," *Third World Quarterly*, April 1990. Ombuds panel from Childers, op. cit., note 12.

60. Macedonia from Paul Lewis, "New Balkans Unit Prepared by U.N.," *New York Times*, November 26, 1992. Tensions between ethnic Hungarians and majorities in the countries they reside in from Jonathan Eyal, "Hungarians Abroad Fear their Hosts' Long-Term Wrath," *The Guardian*, June 13, 1992, from Stephen Engelberg with Judith Ingram, "Now Hungary Adds its Voice to the Ethnic Tumult," *New York Times*, January 25, 1993, and from Gerner, op. cit., note 13. Central Asia from Steven Erlanger, "Tamerlane's Land Trembles: Bloodshed at Gates," *New York Times*, February 15, 1993, and from Barnett R. Rubin, "Afghanistan, Armed and Abandoned, Could be the Next Bosnia" (letter to the editor), *New York Times*, December 28, 1992.

61. Boutros-Ghali, op. cit., note 41. Paul Lewis, "Europeans Urge the U.N. to Act More Aggressively to Prevent War," *New York Times*, September 23, 1992.

62. Johansen, "Lessons," op. cit., note 59; Johansen, "UN Peacekeeping," op. cit., note 59.

63. William Durch, Henry Stimson Center, Washington, D.C., private communication, March 9, 1993.

64. For a detailed discussion, see Gerald B. Helman and Steven R. Ratner, "Saving Failed States," *Foreign Policy*, Winter 1992-93. The authors propose three models of a U.N. "guardianship" role: governance assistance, delegation of governmental authority, and direct trusteeship. As they point out, though, such involvement "should not devolve into a long-term custody." Many war-torn countries need to be rebuilt literally from scratch. For example, in the Mozambique civil war, nearly 1,000 clinics and 3,000 schools were destroyed, and key roads and rail links were damaged or destroyed. See Jane Perlez, "A Mozambique Formally at Peace is Bled by Hunger and Brutality," *New York Times*, October 13, 1992, and John Battersby, "UN Pledges Peacekeepers to Mozambican Cease-Fire," *Christian Science Monitor*, December 18, 1992.

65. Boutros-Ghali, op. cit., note 41; Paul Lewis, "U.N. Chief Seeking 1,000-Troop Units," *New York Times*, June 20, 1992; Paul Lewis, "U.N. Set to Debate Peacemaking Role," *New York Times*, September 6, 1992. Boutros-Ghali's invitation to U.N. member states to "volunteer information about what personnel and equipment they would in principle be ready to contribute, if asked, produced disappointing results." Boutros-Ghali, op. cit., note 48. Scandinavian countries from Åge Eknes, "Vorkämpfer für die Friedenstruppen," *Der Überblick*, September 1992, and from Wolfgang Biermann, "Das Skandinavische Modell für

Friedenserhaltende Maßnahmen," *Frieden und Abrüstung*, October 1992. Denmark, Finland, Norway, and Sweden together have 6,300 trained troops available, a number that may soon rise to 7,000. See Forsvarsdepartmentet (Norwegian Defense Ministry), *Beredskap for Fred. Om Norges Framtidige Militaere FN-engasjement og FNs Rolle som Konfliktloser*, St.meld. nr.14 (1992-93) (Report to Parliament), Oslo, December 18, 1992.

66. Because the U.S. government is potentially the largest contributor of units to U.N. missions, its attitude is of particular interest. Washington has historically refused to place its troops under U.N. command; in a significant departure from past policy, however, the Clinton Administration is putting some (noncombat) U.S. forces in Somalia under command of a U.N. general. The administration insisted, though, that the individual be from Turkey—a member of NATO and a U.S. ally. See R.W. Apple, Jr., "U.N. and the Pentagon," *New York Times*, February 14, 1993.

67. Directly recruited individuals are presumed to have no affiliations with organizations that would question their loyalty to the U.N. To establish a permanent U.N. force, appropriate housing, equipment, and logistics need to be provided. Concerning equipment for communications and transport, the United Nations could initially conclude agreements with national governments to make items available at short notice; at a later stage, the organization might acquire some of the equipment as needed. For a proposal to convert Canadian military facilities to peacekeeping use, see Peter Langille and Erika V. Simpson, "A Training Centre for Peacekeepers," *Ploughshares Monitor*, December 1991.

68. Boutros-Ghali, op. cit., note 48. Lack of in-depth studies from Sommer, op. cit., note 52.

69. Rikhye, op. cit., note 46; Durch and Blechman, op. cit., note 40; Mark Sommer, "Who Should Keep the World's Peace?" *Christian Science Monitor*, August 29, 1991. Scandinavia from Eknes, op. cit., note 65. United States from Thomas L. Friedman, "Bush, in Address to U.N., Urges More Vigor in Keeping Peace," *New York Times*, September 22, 1992. NATO from Hella Pick, "Long Stay for Nato in Bosnia," *The Guardian*, February 20, 1993. Curiously, Canada has developed no training program, even though the country has been involved in almost every U.N. peacekeeping mission. See Langille and Simpson, op. cit., note 67.

70. Norwegian suggestion from "Expanded Norwegian UN-Commitment," Norwegian government press release, No. 135, Oslo, December 18, 1992. A call for regional peacekeeping training centers was made by the Parliamentarians for Global Action in May 1991, as reported by Langille and Simpson, op. cit., note 67. An influential study written by two former high-ranking U.N. officials recommended the creation of a U.N. Staff College, housed at existing universities or other institutions. See Brian Urquhart and Erskine Childers, *A World in Need of Leadership: Tomorrow's United Nations* (Uppsala, Sweden: Dag Hammarskjöld Foundation, 1990).

71. Brian Urquhart, "Foreword," in F.T. Liu, *United Nations Peacekeeping and the Non-Use of Force*, International Peace Academy Occasional Paper Series (Boulder, Colo.: Lynne Rienner Publishers, 1992).

72. Dimitri Simes, "There is No Oil in Bosnia," *New York Times*, March 10, 1993, is exemplary for the argument that there are no strategic interests that dictate Western involvement. The wide divergence of opinions within the peace movement and among grassroots groups is illustrated, for example, by the following articles: "Three Views on the War in Bosnia," *Peace and Democracy News*, Winter 1992/93; Mark Thompson, "No More Evenhandedness," *HCA Newsletter* (Helsinki Citizens' Assembly, Prague), Winter 1993; Jasminka Udovicki, "Bosnian Fantasy," *In These Times*, December 14, 1992.

73. Among the proposals for U.N. rapid deployment forces is one by a commission sponsored by the UNA-USA. See Robert S. Greenberger, "Outspoken U.N. Chief Takes Strong Role, Irking Some Nations," *Wall Street Journal*, December 17, 1992. Boutros-Ghali, op. cit., note 41; Boutros-Ghali, op. cit., note 48.

74. The U.N.'s Congo peacekeeping force in the early 1960s had only a limited right to use force; the Korean war in the early 1950s and the Gulf war against Iraq in 1991 had a nominal U.N. involvement, but the real command was in the hands of U.S. generals. For Somalia, see Lewis, "U.N. Will Increase Troops in Somalia," op. cit., note 43.

75. A two-tier force has been proposed by F.T. Liu, a former U.N. Assistant Secretary-General with responsibility for peacekeeping operations. See Liu, op. cit., note 71.

76. Stevenson quoted in Robert C. Johansen, *Toward a Dependable Peace: A Proposal for an Appropriate Security System*, World Policy Paper No. 8 (New York: World Policy Institute, 1983).

77. De Cuéllar quoted in Paul Lewis, "U.N.'s Fund Crisis Worsens as Role in Security Rises," *New York Times*, January 27, 1992. Thornburgh quoted in "Bungee Jumping at the U.N.," *New York Times*, March 11, 1993.

78. Some 34 countries owed money for only one, two, or three peacekeeping operations out of a total of 14 that are separately budgeted, i.e., not covered by the regular budget. By contrast, some 42 countries owed money for every single one of these missions. Calculated from U.N. Secretariat, "Status of Contributions as at 31 December 1992," ST/ADM/SER.B/395, New York, January 5, 1993.

79. Funding proposals are reported by Schoettle, op. cit., note 44, and by Ann Gertler, "UN Reports on its Varied Roles," *Ploughshares Monitor*, March 1991. In the late 1980s, the General Assembly rejected proposals for borrowing authority and for charging interest. See Durch and Blechman, op. cit., note 40. Brandt Commission from Wulf, op. cit., note 30. Participation in military expenditure reporting from ACDA, op. cit., note 19. China and India are among the larger military powers that have not participated.

80. Durch and Blechman, op. cit., note 40; Boutros-Ghali, op. cit., note 41.

81. Independent Advisory Group on U.N. Financing, op. cit., note 41; Durch and Blechman, op. cit., note 40. The Ford Foundation panel recommends that the Secretary-General be permitted to obligate up to 20 percent of the estimated cost of a peacekeeping operation. Under current rules, no more than $10 million may be obligated before the General Assembly approves a mission budget.

82. U.S. spending for intervention from Joshua Cohen and Joel Rogers, "Central America Policy: The True Cost of Intervention," *The Nation*, April 12, 1986; Salvadoran military spending calculated from Saadet Seger and Somnath Sen, "World Military Expenditure," in SIPRI, op. cit., note 5, and from Saadet Deger, "World Military Expenditure," in SIPRI, *SIPRI Yearbook 1990* (Oxford: Oxford University Press, 1990); number of victims from Heldt, et al., op. cit., note 5; cost of U.N. activities from Table 2. Gulf war from Durch and Blechman, op. cit., note 40.

83. There is no formal link between possession of nuclear weapons and permanent Security Council membership, but the U.K. and French governments have said that they will not relinquish their nuclear arsenal because that might endanger their international status as great powers and thus their hold on a Council seat. See Glenn Frankel, "Britain to Expand Nuclear System," *Washington Post*, January 30, 1992; Bruno Barrillot, "French Finesse Nuclear Future," *Bulletin of the Atomic Scientists*, September 1992.

84. Number of vetoes from Joseph Preston Baratta, "The Veto: Abolition, Modification or Preservation?," in Hoffmann (ed.), op. cit., note 37; Boutros-Ghali quoted in Richard Hudson, "Unilateralism vs. Multilateralism," *Global Report*, Winter 1992-93; the quote was taken from a December 1992 interview of Boutros-Ghali with Leslie Gelb of the *New York Times*. See further Stephen Green, "US Should Avoid Squandering UN's Moral Authority" (Op-Ed), *Christian Science Monitor*, February 12, 1993.

85. China from Baratta, op. cit., note 84.

86. In a candid editorial, the British *Economist* argued that "the veto would be better done away with, and decisions made in a straightforward way on the basis of a two-thirds majority." But abolition of the veto is resisted because "its possession guards self-important governments from the prospect of being obliged by lesser folk to do something they do not want to do." See "Open the Club," *Economist*, August 29, 1992.

87. Proposal for gradually relinquishing the veto from Baratta, op. cit., note 84.

88. Paul Lewis, "West Acts to Defer Issue of New U.N. Council Seats," *New York Times*, January 3, 1992; Paul Lewis, "Germany Tells the U.N. It Wants a Permanent Seat on the Council," *New York Times*, September 24, 1992. For the suggestion of regional seats, see Samantha Pelosi, "Broadening the Mandate of the Security Council, Reviewing the Composition of the Security Council and the Use of the Veto," in Walter Hoffmann (ed.), *Rethinking Basic Assumptions About the United Nations*, Briefing Booklet (Washington, D.C.: World Federalist Association, November 1992). The current permanent Council members account for about two-thirds of world military spending (1989), slightly less than half of global GNP (1989), and about one-third of world population (1991). Adding the other six potential candidates would bring the share accounted for by the permanent members to 74, 71, and 60 percent, respectively. Worldwatch Institute, calculated from ACDA, op. cit., note 19, and from Population Reference Bureau, *World Population Data Sheet 1991* (Washington, D.C.: PRB, 1991).

89. The discussion in Germany and Japan is intense. On Germany, see Oliver Thränert, "Germans Battle Over Blue Helmets," *Bulletin of the Atomic Scientists*,

October 1992, Rainer Kern, "Zur Diskussion um Out-of-Area-Einsätze der Bundeswehr," *Frieden und Abrüstung,* October 1992, and Quentin Peel, "Bonn Agrees Formula for Joining UN Forces," *Financial Times,* January 14, 1993; on Japan, see *The Strengthening of the U.N. Peace Function and Japan's Role* (Tokyo: The Japan Forum on International Relations, October 1992), David E. Sanger, "Japan's Parliament Votes to End Ban on Sending Troops Abroad," *New York Times,* June 16, 1992, David E. Sanger, "Japanese Discuss Widened Military," *New York Times,* January 10, 1993, and David E. Sanger, "Japanese Debate Taboo Topic of Military's Role," *New York Times,* January 17, 1993.

90. Laurenti, op. cit., note 39. Among the few countries that have not been involved in wars in recent decades are Costa Rica, Venezuela, Iceland, Sweden, Switzerland, and Côte d'Ivoire, but Sweden and Switzerland have significant domestic arms industries and export substantial amounts of military equipment. For data on war involvement, see Sivard, op. cit., note 6; for data on armed forces and arms exports, see ACDA, op. cit., note 19; for data on arms industries, see Michael Renner, *Economic Adjustments after the Cold War: Strategies for Conversion* (Aldershot, UK: Dartmouth Publishing Co., 1992).

91. Establishing a "binding triad" would require amending Articles 13 and 18 of the U.N. Charter. Hudson argues that no country should contribute more than 15 percent of the regular U.N. budget to avoid any nations exercising too much influence; the United States currently is assessed 25 percent of the regular budget, and 30.4 percent of peacekeeping budgets. Richard Hudson, "Should There Be a Global Parliament? What Is the Binding Triad?," in Hoffmann (ed.), op. cit., note 37. U.S. share from Durch and Blechman, op. cit., note 40.

92. The idea of a second chamber is discussed by Ron Glossop, "Should There be a UN Parliamentary Assembly and/or Direct Popular Election of UN Delegates?," in Hoffmann (ed.), op. cit., note 37.

93. Serbs make up almost 12 percent of the population of Croatia and 31.5 percent of that of Bosnia, but only 2 percent of Slovenia. Croats account for 17 percent of Bosnia's population. Sabrina Petra Ramet, "Balkan Wars," *Foreign Affairs,* Fall 1992; Markotic et al., op. cit., note 15; Friends Committee on National Legislation, *FCNL Washington Newsletter,* November 1992.

94. In March 1992, the Scandinavian countries recommended to the Secretary-General that pools of experts be created. See Biermann, op. cit., note 66.

THE WORLDWATCH PAPER SERIES

_____100. **Beyond the Petroleum Age: Designing a Solar Economy** by Christopher Flavin and Nicholas Lenssen.

_____101. **Discarding the Throwaway Society** by John E. Young.

_____102. **Women's Reproductive Health: The Silent Emergency** by Jodi L. Jacobson.

_____103. **Taking Stock: Animal Farming and the Environment** by Alan B. Durning and Holly B. Brough.

_____104. **Jobs in a Sustainable Economy** by Michael Renner.

_____105. **Shaping Cities: The Environmental and Human Dimensions** by Marcia D. Lowe.

_____106. **Nuclear Waste: The Problem That Won't Go Away** by Nicholas Lenssen.

_____107. **After the Earth Summit: The Future of Environmental Governance** by Hilary F. French.

_____108. **Life Support: Conserving Biological Diversity** by John C. Ryan.

_____109. **Mining the Earth** by John E. Young.

_____110. **Gender Bias: Roadblock to Sustainable Development** by Jodi L. Jacobson.

_____111. **Empowering Development: The New Energy Equation** by Nicholas Lenssen.

_____112. **Guardians of the Land: Indigenous Peoples and the Health of the Earth** by Alan Thein Durning.

_____113. **Costly Tradeoffs: Reconciling Trade and the Environment** by Hilary F. French.

_____114. **Critical Juncture: The Future of Peacekeeping** by Michael Renner.

_____ **Total Copies**

☐ **Single Copy: $5.00**
☐ **Bulk Copies (any combination of titles)**
   ☐ 2–5: $4.00 ea.   ☐ 6–20: $3.00 ea.   ☐ 21 or more: $2.00 ea.

☐ **Membership in the Worldwatch Library: $25.00 (international airmail $40.00)**
The paperback edition of our 250-page "annual physical of the planet," *State of the World 1993*, plus all Worldwatch Papers released during the calendar year.

☐ **Subscription to *World Watch* Magazine: $15.00 (international airmail $30.00)**
Stay abreast of global environmental trends and issues with our award-winning, eminently readable bimonthly magazine.

No postage required on prepaid orders. Minimum $3 postage and handling charge on unpaid orders.

Make check payable to Worldwatch Institute
1776 Massachusetts Avenue, N.W., Washington, D.C. 20036-1904 USA

Enclosed is my check for U.S. $_____

_____

name   **daytime phone #**

_____

address

_____

city   **state**   **zip/country**